THE RESTLESS GHOSTS OF LADYE PLACE
and other True Hauntings

THE RESTLESS GHOSTS
OF LADYE PLACE

and other True Hauntings

by

HARRY LUDLAM

TAPLINGER PUBLISHING COMPANY
NEW YORK

First published in the United States in 1968 by

TAPLINGER PUBLISHING CO., INC.
29 East Tenth Street
New York, New York 10003

THE RESTLESS GHOSTS
OF LADYE PLACE

© *Harry Ludlam 1967*

Library of Congress Catalog Card Number: 68 - 31250

Made and Printed in Great Britain

FOR MARY AND GENE

CONTENTS

I am grateful to the many people who freely helped in the preparation of this book, and whose names are given in the stories concerning them. I would also like to express my deep appreciation of the valuable assistance given by Paul Lund, Robert V. Steele, Charlotte E. Tucker, Gladys Cordwell, and Emma Macdonald.

H.L.

THE GHOST OF SARAH THORNE

On a July day in 1874 the rebuilt Theatre Royal, Margate, opened its doors under the new management of a woman. She was Sarah Thorne, a well known actress in her thirties, who gave the century-old theatre a busy and colourful new lease of life. She had been, as *The Times* later observed, "a useful member of various companies, her talents being rather of the 'sound' than the brilliant order". For some time on assuming the management she took leading parts in plays presented at the Theatre Royal, but she then found the ideal outlet for her talents in setting up a training school for young would-be actors and actresses.

Sarah Thorne reigned at the theatre for twenty years, living for much of this time just across the square in a home built by Nelson for Lady Hamilton. Her school of acting became famous. She put her pupils through an intensive course of tuition and practice on the old "stock system" principle, also sending out companies on tour throughout the southern counties. From her school came many leading actors and actresses of later years, among them the Vanbrugh sisters, Irene and Violet, George Arliss and his wife, and Sir Seymour Hicks and his wife.

The late Dame Irene Vanbrugh, who made her debut at the Theatre Royal at the age of fifteen, recalled, "What a teacher Sarah Thorne was. She was not a good actress and her appearance did not help her, but the ability to teach others—that was a real gift."

Sarah died tragically on February 27, 1899 from a severe attack of influenza, just as leading theatre personalities were about to celebrate her stage jubilee with a special performance at the St James's Theatre, London. She died, aged 62, at her home in Chatham, where in later years she had also acquired the lease of the Chatham Opera House; but her heart remained in Margate. When dying she was heard to declare, "So long as the Theatre Royal is there, I shall be there."

During the following years there were a number of strange incidents at the theatre which led some people to believe that

Sarah had indeed kept her vow and returned to haunt the place she loved. The witnesses of various unaccountable noises and, from time to time, a "filmy form", included theatre staff, actors, and Sarah Thorne's son (she was married to Mr Thomas MacKnight, a journalist). He told several people of his seeing the wraith of his mother, among them N. V. Norman, who in the 1930s recalled: "I used to send companies to Margate and play there a great deal, and I remember Mr MacKnight emphatically telling me that he had many times seen the ghost of his mother. My wife (Miss Beatrice Withers) who as a young girl was a pupil of Sarah Thorne, has heard Mr MacKnight say the same thing."

That there should be such firm evidence about the existence of Sarah's ghost was doubly surprising because the theatre had already received the attentions of one ghostly figure. This was believed to be the spirit of a demented actor of the last century, who, on being summarily dismissed, bought himself a box for the next night's performance and during the course of the play leapt from the box to the orchestra pit, breaking his neck. After the turn of the century this actor's ghost was seen to appear sitting motionless in the box on so many occasions that the management eventually had to withdraw it from sale and leave it always curtained. Even then the actor's apparition was seen to continue to draw aside the curtains during a performance, one of the many witnesses of this phenomenon being the late W. J. Macqueen-Pope, the theatre historian. The haunting ceased when the boxes were finally bricked up as part of new fire precautions in the theatre, when an escape tower with spiral staircase was built at that side of the stage; but this work was only done in recent years.

In the 1920s and early 1930s, however, Sarah Thorne's ghost provided the more poignant haunting at the theatre, though few people at the time cared to speak openly about it, which was why in April, 1934 when Mr Caspar Middleton took over the lease of the Theatre Royal, he knew nothing at all of its ghostly background. He was, in any case, strongly sceptical of such matters. Yet within weeks he had seen the ghost, not once but three times. This was his later testimony:

"Twice on coming out of the circle buffet some time after the performance I saw it walk though the doorway from the stairs leading to the boxes and gallery on one side, and go slowly round the back of the circle and disappear through a wall on the other side. At one time there was an opening in this wall with stairs leading down to the stage, and I am told that Sarah Thorne had a small office on the side of the stage which could be approached from these stairs.

"On one occasion the ghost passed so close that I could almost have reached it with my hand. On another night I was standing in the circle, when I saw it by the door in the stalls leading to the boxes."

The ghost, according to Mr Middleton, wore clothes similar to the accepted sleep-walking dress of the stage Lady Macbeth—bluish-grey draperies, flowing and transparent. He did not immediately say anything about what he had seen but asked a few patrons of the theatre about its history, and made inquiries among several old residents of Margate. Even when he had established that the threatre was strongly believed to be haunted, he kept silent. What finally made the whole affair public was the alarming experience of two unsuspecting actresses very shortly afterwards.

On the night of August 22, 1934 members of the theatre's new repertory company were rehearsing at midnight for their opening performance of "The Naughty Lady", and as the stage was laid out for use by the company appearing that week, the rehearsal was being held in the circle buffet. One of the actresses, Miss Peggy Ford-Carrington, left the buffet and stood under a small gaslight at the side of the circle, reading her part. The rest of the theatre was in darkness, with the fireproof curtain down on the silent stage. In her own words: "Suddenly I was startled by a gentle moan or cry which broke the stillness, and glancing up I saw something leaning over the box on the other side, waving its arms about. It was terrifying and I could not stop myself from screaming. Chic (Miss Chic Elliott, another actress) came rushing out, and immediately she saw it she fainted. I could not take my eyes off it. . . ."

Next out of the buffet on hearing the scream was Mr Middleton. "I immediately looked across the theatre, and, in the circle box, saw something swaying and waving over the edge. Despite what I had previously seen I tried to think it was some practical joke, yet I could not understand how anyone could have entered the place to carry it out, and the door to the stage itself was locked. I immediately ran round the circle, through the door from which I had previously seen the ghost appear, and into the box. No one was there and nothing had been disturbed."

While Mr Middleton was running round to the box Miss Ford-Carrington was held transfixed by the apparition—a bluish-grey transparent figure of a woman—and to her continued amazement saw it gradually rise into the air over the front of the box and disappear into the theatre roof.

Now that the haunting was made public other evidence in support was forthcoming, and it seemed clear that the ghost's practice was to make a tour of the circle, just as Sarah Thorne had done after every evening performance, disappearing at the spot where her office had been. Investigators who held a night's vigil, however, saw nothing.

There was an unexpected development when Sister E. Thorne of Harrow, a niece of Sarah Thorne, on hearing of the renewed ghostly activity at the Theatre Royal called and told the lessee that it might not, after all, be her famous aunt who was responsible for the haunting. Many people had believed in the ghost as far back as the 1890s, said Sister Thorne, and Sarah herself had often described how she encountered a supernatural figure wearing a grey habit, in a vault beneath the theatre. The vault, formed by a subterranean passage which then ran under the street, was believed to date from a Catholic retreat that stood on the site long before the theatre was built. Sister Thorne said that her aunt, using this passageway one day, came face to face with the apparition and promptly fainted, lying helpless in the vault for some three or four hours before being found.

So this posed the question, *was* the apparition recently seen that of Sarah Thorne? Wearing, perhaps, the dress she had used when playing Lady Macbeth? Or was it the figure the actress herself had seen, gowned in a blue-grey costume like that of a nun? The evidence was not at all conclusive.

During the following years there were more reports of inexplicable happenings at the theatre; mainly strange noises and half-seen ghostly shapes. The ghosts remained with the theatre through a chequered career which saw it used for repertory. twice-nightly revue, wrestling, and even as a cinema. The theatre closed during World War II when badly damaged by a bomb that fell nearby. In 1948, the year of its reopening—and the year in which Dame Irene Vanbrugh, celebrating her diamond jubilee on the stage, returned to tread the boards where her apprenticeship had begun—manifestations were seen again. Late one night just before the reopening in July, phenomena occurred of which the chief features were the prolonged screams of a terrified woman and the sound of footsteps hurrying across the empty stage. Mr Robert G. Butler, the theatre's managing director, and no fewer than thirteen other people testified to this weird occurrence.

Another phenomenon reported at the theatre was a mysterious orange ball of light. This, first seen in the auditorium and scarcely bigger than a marble, travelled over the footlights and across the stage, growing to the size of a football before disappearing through the passage to the stage door.

Later, in 1954, two frightened workmen who stayed on late one night doing repairs at the theatre, said that just as they were preparing to leave they heard, in the circle overhead, the sound of agitated pacing. The ghost, however, was not visible. Early the following year the assistant stage manager told of the theatre's heavy front doors being unbolted twice in the early hours, and of the foyer lights blazing on hours after they had been put out. There was, he said, a general feeling of eeriness about the place. The caretaker at the time supported this, adding that frequently after turning out the gaslights backstage he found them on again some time later. Often, he said, the sensation of uneasiness in the theatre at night was almost overwhelming.

So the theatre hauntings persisted through several changes of management into the 1960s, when, after a period of quiet, the ghost or ghosts became suddenly very active once more.

In January, 1966 Mr Alfred Tanner, who was not a local man and knew nothing about the theatre's history, undertook to paint the auditorium for the lessee, Mr Harry Jacobs. He began work at 10 pm. on a Sunday night, working through alone in the theatre till 6.30 am., and several times during the night thought he heard "coughing and whispering". Puzzled, he searched the building but could find nothing to account for the noises. The following night, as he later told the *Isle of Thanet Gazette:* "At about 1.30 am. I heard the booking office door slam. When I investigated the door was wide open. A few minutes later I heard a backstage door slam heavily. I went to look and found it was closed and bolted, as it was when I started work."

Then, as he was standing by the entrance to the auditorium, there suddenly came into his startled view what seemed to be a disembodied female head.

"It came round the curtains on the left of the stage. It was just a head and neck, with a lot of frizzy hair, two slits for eyes and a thin, receding chin. It was the head and shoulders of a woman. I watched it for a few seconds moving across the stage before it disappeared."

His eyes were then drawn to another door of the auditorium, where a set of heavy curtains had been lifted clear of the wall and folded on a large semi-circular wooden pelmet.

"I saw the curtains lift up and then slowly drop down as if someone was lifting them down from the pelmet. I went to the door, and as I lifted the curtains I felt an odd sensation at the back of my neck, as if someone was staring at me, and my hair started to bristle."

It was then that Mr Tanner decided he had had enough. He

locked up the theatre and went home, but was so shaken that he
could not sleep and sat up the rest of the night reading.

On returning to the theatre next morning Mr Tanner, as he was
going upstairs with a colleague, stopped suddenly by an old
photograph of Sarah Thorne dressed in her sleep-walking costume
for "Macbeth".

"That's the face I saw last night!" he exclaimed.

Mr Tanner refused on any account to work alone again in the
theatre at night. Mr Jacobs, the lessee, told me, "I did not know
what to make of his story; after all, one might expect a very old
theatre to be full of noises at night. The main thing was that the
painting should be finished, so I suggested to Mr Tanner that he
took someone with him for company on the third night, and he
finally agreed to this."

The man who accompanied Mr Tanner was Mr Lawrence John
Rodgers, of Margate, who, like his companion, knew nothing of
the theatre's ghostly history. Mr Rodgers afterwards described
how, when they were both in the auditorium, strange noises
culminated in "a terrific crash, as if something very heavy had
been thrown into the stalls from the balcony. We went to the spot
where the noise came from but could find nothing."

At this Mr Tanner gave up and went home, but Mr Rodgers
went along to the police station to report the strange happenings,
with the result that at 2 am. eight policemen searched the theatre
from top to bottom but failed to find anything that would account
for the noises.

Mr Tanner, summing up his alarming three nights in the building, told the *Isle of Thanet Gazette:* "All the time I was in the theatre
I experienced the same feeling I had during the war when I used
to go out on night patrol in the desert in the Eighth Army—a
feeling that someone or something was always behind you and
that something awful was going to happen."

An interested reader of the *Gazette* report of these most recent
hauntings, published on the morning of Friday, January 28, 1966
was Mr James H. Chell, a Margate teacher who had for some years
studied psychical research. Mr Chell immediately sought and was
given permission to keep observation in the theatre that night. He
duly arrived at the theatre with his dog to be told that there was
now another man who wished to keep a vigil—would he agree to
them keeping watch in company? Mr Chell agreed to this, and so
he and Mr Thomas Redshaw of Margate, who had not met before,
prepared for their vigil. After the bingo sessions were finished for
the day the two men searched the building thoroughly to make
sure that no practical jokers had been at work. Then, after en-

suring that all external doors were secure and not capable of being opened from the outside, they turned off the electric lights at the big switches situated on a high platform behind the stage backcloth. This left the theatre in darkness except for two small gaslights, one on each side of the auditorium.

Mr Chell now gives his concise record of what followed:

"We began our vigil at about 12.30 am. After half an hour there was a sudden coldness and a noise sounded behind the stage backcloth, as though several large pieces of furniture were being dragged about. My dog, which had been silent till then, began to howl; her hackles went up, something which I had not seen in her before, nor have I since.

"I investigated the noises but found nothing at all behind the backcloth; no furniture, boxes or anything. Returning to my seat I began to eat the sandwiches I had brought. At about 1.35 it again went intensely cold; then there was a loud explosion and all the lights in the auditorium came on. I immediately went with Mr Redshaw to the platform behind the backcloth, climbed the ladder and saw that the heavy iron-clad light switches, which we had switched off, were now back in the 'ON' position. Human hands could never have switched on *all three* of these switches simultaneously; even were a man to find the strength to do so, he would need three hands to operate them all at once.

"We searched all through the building again, going up the spiral stairs ascending a tower at the side of the stage where formerly three boxes existed. At the top of this staircase we noticed a smell as though there were dead leaves present, and after a few minutes this smell changed to one of roses. Again we experienced a wave of intense cold, which despite the fact that the building was centrally-heated was very unpleasant. As before, the cold disappeared with the passing of the event.

"At about 2.30 there was another explosion and all the lights went out again. On re-inspecting the light switches I found they had now been returned to the 'OFF' position. Returning to my seat in the front stalls I began to make a note of what had occurred and was suddenly aware of the ticking of a large clock, which lasted for exactly four minutes. I knew there was no clock in the theatre and later found that none had existed in the building within living memory.

"Nothing more occurred until about 3.15, when I became aware of a large patch on the wall where, years ago, there had existed a box, which was now bricked in and the wall painted blue. The patch, which was dirty brown in colour, moved slightly, then disappeared. I thought it might be my imagination at first, but

when the 'thing' appeared a second time I knew it to be a fact.
It remained for about 30 seconds and then vanished.

"During all this time there were various shufflings and scratchings in the theatre but I knew it was hopeless to try and track the
source of them.

"At 3.55 I thought I would try and have a nap, as our vigil had
been rather a strain, so I took a blanket from the organ in front
of the stage, put my bag under my head and settled down. It was
then two minutes to four. I awoke suddenly to find Mr Redshaw
absent. Hearing a noise from the first gallery, I looked up and saw
him trying to light a match and walking slowly forward. On seeing
I had woken up he came down and asked if I had heard a bump.
I said I had not, but that something had woken me. It was three
minutes past four; I had fallen asleep immediately and slept for
only five minutes.

"Mr Redshaw asked for my torch, but as I handed it to him I
thought I could 'feel' something in the vicinity of the first gallery,
so I turned and shone the torch towards the gallery, where, in the
beam of light, I saw the same brown shape as before. It hung
around near one of the slim pillars supporting the gallery and then
glided towards the next pillar where it suddenly disappeared,
again accompanied by the wave of intense cold. We searched the
building together, and when we came to the spot where we had
seen the brown shape, the place felt evil.

"It was now about 4.30 and we decided to leave. We locked the
door quietly as we left and walked up the road towards the main
road. We had been walking for some time, well out of earshot of
the theatre, when we were suddenly caught up with by a policeman on a motor-cycle. He asked us our business and, when we
told him, what time we had left the theatre. He then said that only
fifteen minutes ago someone living near the theatre had heard a
loud explosion coming from the building and telephoned the
police station. We had heard nothing, so the explosion must have
taken place *after* we had left the building."

The ghost of Sarah Thorne, it appears, is scarcely alone in her
beloved theatre.

THE RESTLESS GHOSTS OF LADYE PLACE

When he retired from the Royal Engineers in his late thirties, wealthy Lieutenant-Colonel Charles Noel Rivers-Moore looked around for a small country estate on which he and his wife could settle. He eventually found the ideal place at Hurley, East Berkshire, in the valley of the River Thames; Ladye Place, an historic building standing in twenty acres of land.

The year was 1924. The grey pile of Ladye Place, girdled by its silver moat, rose through the trees at the end of a quiet lane set well away from the roads around Maidenhead. Though the big house was scarcely a century old, its foundations and other buildings and remains close by went back many hundreds of years.

Colonel Rivers-Moore had in fact come as near as any man to owning a piece of English history, for Ladye Place had begun life shortly after the Norman Conquest as a small Benedictine priory. The Colonel had of course learned something of its background; a handful of histories of Hurley and Ladye Place had been written in recent years, and the previous owner had even put up some explanatory tablets on different parts of the buildings, and published a little guidebook. On moving in the Colonel and his wife, Barbara, keenly read up every account of the place they could lay hands on, and this same year the Colonel, who had developed a great interest in archaeology, joined the Berkshire Archaeological Society.

Ghosts? Yes, there were many hints locally of phantoms reputed to haunt Ladye Place, but the Colonel was not concerned with these. His studies over the next few years were conducted exclusively into the historical past of the fascinating old property he had acquired.

Ladye Place, when he bought it, could be summarized in the dull language of the estate agent as comprising twenty acres of land with long river and road frontages, and containing a main residence with thirteen bedrooms, five bathrooms and four reception rooms; also two secondary residences and two cottages. But this bald description took no account of the living history there

B

which included, among several ancient buildings and ruins, the old parish church of Hurley.

The Colonel found in his enthusiastic researches that the Domesday Book contained first mention of the estate, referring to a one-time Hurley Manor which had belonged to Easgar, Master of the Horse to King Edward the Confessor. A church had existed on the site even then. On the Norman Conquest, Easgar's lands were given to Geoffrey de Mandeville, who founded St Mary's Priory there in 1086. Some of the existing buildings, and most of the church, dated from this time.

After Henry VIII swept the monks out of St Mary's Priory in the dissolution of 1536 the land eventually was bought by the Lovelace family. In 1600 Richard Lovelace, first Baron of Hurley, built a great Elizabethan mansion—Ladye Place—on the site of the Priory, converting the monks' refectory or dining hall into stables and a hayloft for his horses. This mansion stood for more than two centuries, falling eventually into such decay that in 1837 it was demolished, and the present house built in its place.

Colonel Rivers-Moore was eager to commence digging right away in an attempt to uncover the various mysteries of Ladye Place, which, although written about, was archaeologically almost completely untouched. He hoped to disclose the early foundation work and chart the ancient buildings as they had once existed: also to retrieve whatever archaeological treasures may lie buried under the rebuildings and restorations of centuries. He was particularly intrigued by a charter dated the 15th year of Richard II, which mentioned that Editha, sister of Edward the Confessor, was buried there. One of his cherished objects was to try and find the grave of Editha, for it was her ghost—the Grey Lady—that was locally claimed to haunt Ladye Place, along with the spectre of William Rufus, who was once known there, and the sombre spirits of the monks who had prayed in the cloisters of the old Priory.

But where was he to begin excavations? The buildings of Ladye Place were grouped round a courtyard partly occupying the site of the original cloister yard. On the south side of this quadrangle was the old parish church, and on the north side the converted refectory and a large Tudor barn, to which had recently been added a garage and schoolroom.

On the eastern side of the courtyard was a building which had always been known as "Paradise". This was a secondary house believed to have been rebuilt in the 17th century on the actual cloister foundations. Its upper windows at each end, now blocked, had once looked respectively into the church and the refectory.

Detached from this group of buildings and shaded by a great cedar said to have been planted in the days of the Crusaders, was the remaining portion of the old crypt which Lovelace had used as the cellar of his mansion, while other buildings still standing included a tythe barn and dove-cote both erected in 1306.

The present main residence of Ladye Place had been rebuilt round the old farmhouse of the Priory, and parts of it still dated from the 16th century. One stroke of luck for the Colonel was the advent of an exceptionally dry season, which caused the foundation outline of Lovelace's vanished mansion to appear through the turf of the lawn and allow him accurately to trace its dimensions. Between 1924 and 1930, however, being unsure of where to start, he attempted no serious excavation beyond digging a trial pit against a corner of the church, to see if the walls had once extended at that point. It was his first move in the search for Editha's grave. But three feet down he struck a flat floor or pavement of hard chalk, and gave up. What made it so much harder to find the early walls of the church was that at the last restoration both the ground around the church and the church floor itself had been raised some three feet because of flood trouble.

It was shortly after this abortive effort that the slowly awakening ghosts of Ladye Place seemed to take a hand.

The strange sequence of events began in the early spring of 1930, when Mrs Rivers-Moore's brother, a doctor on the staff of a London hospital, came to stay. One day he told them he had had a surprising "vision" in which he seemed to be in the dining room of "Paradise", talking to a monk dressed in a brown habit. He remarked to the monk that it was a pity about the fireplace in the room as it was not in keeping with the house. The monk, by way of reply, said three times, "Sweep it away," making a sweeping motion with his hand—and to the doctor the fireplace then seemed to fade away, revealing behind it a semi-circular fireplace surmounted by a big oak beam.

Next day, out of curiosity Mrs Rivers-Moore asked some builders who were then working in the house to remove the offending fireplace. To everyone's astonishment, when they took it out there was disclosed behind it a much older fireplace exactly as described by her brother.

From this time on the ghostly incidents at Ladye Place rapidly gathered momentum. A woman visitor who stayed at "Paradise" had some strange experiences in the house which, she felt sure, indicated the presence of unseen forces. She decided to take some instruction on psychic research in London, and on returning to "Paradise" tried experimenting with automatic writing. One day she came to the Colonel and his wife with a paper on which was written "Empty well". As they did not know of any well about the place, however, this puzzling "message" meant little. Then, shortly afterwards, their guest brought another scrawl produced by automatic writing which seemed to be a drawing of a well and three arches of the old Priory.

Feeling that there might be something to this allegedly psychic phenomena after all, Colonel Rivers-Moore and his wife, together with a few friends, decided to try a table-rapping seance in the hope of gaining information. The seance was conducted with perfectly open mind and with no medium or spiritualist present, the simple procedure being that the table should give one rap for "No" and two raps for "Yes". They found the table very quickly responsive and were soon obtaining answers from a spirit or entity who gave his name as "King" and said he had lived 400 years ago. The sitters asked "King" about the mysterious well, and he replied that there was such a well 13 feet south from a corner of the church and six feet east, and that it was filled with rubbish.

The Colonel, after six somewhat impatient years at Ladye Place, was willing to take a gamble, and so on April 23, 1930 he began digging where instructed; but all he found was the remains of an old flint wall. Another table-rapping seance was held and "King" then told him that he should dig two feet farther south. He did this, and then found the well exactly as described, filled with building debris. After clearing it for some depth he struck water and work was suspended, though he had now, under guidance, uncovered the foundation of the Tudor mansion and unearthed a few relics including the foot of a skeleton.

There were more table-rapping seances and Mrs Rivers-Moore, seeking a special test for "King", asked the spirit, "Can you tell me something we can find in the morning that nobody knows is there?" The answer came "Look for the rust line." Next morning her husband quite easily found a rust line just under the surface of the ground where they had been excavating, at the precise spot indicated.

The messages received by table-rapping continued to be so explicit that relics were unearthed within a few hours of a seance. The well, two old fireplaces and hidden foundations were all discovered by this means. The Colonel pressed on for two years with the work, amassing little treasures as he went: 13th-century floor tiling from the church and Priory, old church carvings, pottery, 17th-century smoking pipes, a skull and other remains. He began a unique museum in the old musicians' gallery of the ancient refectory.

The Colonel also rediscovered and cleared out a "secret passage" leading from the moat to the cellar of Ladye Place. The cellar had been constructed over the monks' burial ground, and skeletons had since been dug from its floor. It was here in this cellar, in the bloodless revolution of 1688, that the Whig plotters against James II had met at the request of the third Lord Lovelace and decided to invite William of Orange to the English throne. Through the "secret passage" from the moat, which was in fact a sewer to the mansion, had crept the revolutionaries gathering for their midnight conferences.

So far as the Colonel and his friends were able to make out at the seances, "King", who had lived at the time of the dissolution of the monastery, had stolen some jewels and thrown them down the well which he had directed them to find. The Colonel, however, having by the spring of 1932 got down to river level, working up to his waist in water in the old well, had little hopes of ever probing the bottom of it, even though the table-messages urged that it should be emptied so that the spirit of the Grey Lady could find peace. There had also been conversations, meantime, with a monk named Edipus, who had lived about the year 1200. In fact the phantoms of Ladye Place had really become alive, for several guests who stayed there, some among them the strongest of sceptics, confessed to psychic experiences including the sight of spectral monks. All this made the Colonel and his wife more inclined to give credit to the reports of people who, in the past, had claimed to have seen the apparitions of William Rufus and the Grey Lady.

In April, 1932 Colonel Rivers-Moore and his wife, at the invitation of friends, described at a drawing-room meeting in Reading the remarkable psychic guidance they had been given in their excavations so far at Ladye Place. The Colonel, not for the first time, stressed, "We have had no so-called mediums or spiritualists at all, but have conducted proceedings entirely on our own. We are not spiritualists but have quite open minds on the subject." A former vicar of Hurley who was present at the little gathering said there must be some great good to come out of what was happening and there was no knowing what would be the end of it.

Indeed, as the years went by there seemed no end. Throughout the 1930s the Colonel, freely enlisting the help of friends, fellow members of the Berkshire Archaeological Society and others interested to help dig or research and classify his mounting collection, pursued his investigations of the old Priory with singular dedication, having a devoted helpmate in his wife. A

second old well was discovered, though after much effort to drain
the water from both wells nothing of interest was found. No jewels.
The wells had obviously been cleaned out when Lovelace's mansion was built. Editha's grave, too, upon the discovery of which the
Colonel had placed so much hope, eluded him. He had vowed he
would search for the Grey Lady's resting place if it meant ruining
the grounds, but although many graves were struck and some
mixed bones and other grisly relics uncovered, all that came to
light that could possibly be connected with Editha was a base of
hard core surrounded by traces of tile flooring, in the centre of the
north transept of the church. This may well have formed the base
of some early shrine.

The Colonel did succeed in laying bare other secrets of the
Priory. He uncovered almost all the foundations of the monastic
church, chapter house, part of the cloister, and a range of buildings north of the church. His discoveries brought such new light
on the buildings that he had to take down some of the tablets
put up by the previous occupier as they were so obviously in-
correct. The contents of his museum swelled. And during all this
work the ghosts of Ladye Place grew steadily more restless.

A woman who for a time occupied "Paradise" with her child
became convinced there was an evil influence in the building. She
was advised to sprinkle holy water in the rooms. But just as she
was about to do this, the warning apparition of a monk appeared
to her and said, "You must not do it—you will stop my work."
A medium was brought in, but as soon as he went into a trance
the monk took possession and became violent, trying to attack the
sitters. Through the medium the monk declared that he had
practised black magic, and ever since had tried to keep his per-
secutors out of the house. He was assured by the circle that he had
been forgiven by his Father Prior, whereupon he promised not to
cause further difficulty in the house.

Other shades, however, began to appear. Spectral monks of the
old Priory were seen by friends and visitors to Ladye Place many
dozens of times during the 1930s. Commonly a visitor walking in
the cloisters in the early evening would see a man dressed in
monk's habit, with arms crossed, pass him and then vanish before
his eyes. Colonel Rivers-Moore and his wife compiled a dossier
of the weird happenings, each story being signed by the witnesses.
The signatures included those of an architect, a doctor, and
prosaic-minded officers of the Navy, Army and Air Force.

For nine years the Colonel and various helpers were busy
digging at Ladye Place; he then finished the remaining work alone
or with an occasional companion. In the 1940s, when he had been

more than twenty years on the estate, he had wrested from it practically every archaeological secret—except the last resting place of the Grey Lady. In the spring of 1947 he took members of Berkshire Archaeological Society on a last excursion to Ladye Place, and in the autumn he put it up for auction, "A Small Country Estate of Great Historical Interest. . . ."

His work was there for all to see. The prospective buyer could walk the haunted grounds, peer into secret passages and climb the creaking stairs to look into the cloisters of the old monastery. He could, the *Maidenhead Advertiser* reported, walk "lawns full of mystery. On the one leading to the old monks' fish pond is the wooden lid of a vault. Lift it and you will see a skeleton. Buried near the crypt is the body of a man, accidentally disinterred, wearing the robes of a monastic order. Near him lies a local giant. Under the lawn is a subterranean passage approached through a trapdoor. The foundations of the chapel built in 1086 can be traced and you can walk on pieces of the original floor. There is a glass case round the foundations of the chapter house so that the historical features may be seen. A reconstruction of the old Priory is in the museum reached from the gallery in the magnificent refectory hall. . . ."

Museum, furniture and effects were all included in the sale, but Ladye Place did not reach its reserve price and was sold shortly afterwards in pieces; the cloisters, chapter house, monks' parlour and refectory together; the land for farming as a market garden; the mansion itself for conversion into three homes.

Colonel Rivers-Moore moved to Wargrave, Berkshire, where he remained for some years and joined in other local archaeological work. Following the death of his wife, and remarriage, he moved to Scotland, where he died at Elgin in 1965.

The restless ghosts of Ladye Place had quietened long before.

GO AWAY SAMUEL GREATREX

Widowed Mrs Kathleen Keogh noticed something strange about her Corporation-owned home in the Small Heath district of Birmingham, immediately she moved into it, in the summer of 1963. It was an old back-to-back house in Garrison Lane, set among rows of similar houses eventually to disappear under city clearance schemes, and had one bedroom, with an attic above. Mrs Keogh, on going up into the bedroom found it to be abnormally cold.

There was, however, little she could do about this, so she prepared the room for sleeping in with her five-year-old son in a double bed. Within a week she received a tremendous shock, awaking one night to hear an eerie noise like a man finding it difficult to breathe, and a voice saying "My God, my God. . . ". The ghostly sounds seemed to issue from the exact spot in the bed where she lay—*coming from and through herself.*

This experience so frightened her that she never slept upstairs again, using instead a bed settee downstairs, with her young son. But it was only the start of her ordeal. A mirror hung by a chain on the bedroom wall began to rattle at night; she constantly heard the chain rapping against the wall. Then came sounds of footsteps on the stairs, usually at night, and a series of uncanny knockings, both upstairs in the bedroom and downstairs in the living room. It was just as if someone was rapping sharply with the knuckles, mainly on the furniture.

Mrs Keogh had no belief in ghosts and had seldom even thought about them. She was a devout Catholic and had many religious ornaments about the house. She tried to make the best of her accommodation, working hard to make the little house comfortable, but the brooding atmosphere, the mysterious footsteps and the knockings persisted. On more than one occasion they so terrified her that she left the house at night and walked the streets with her son asleep in her arms; she was afraid to tell the neighbours about the noises in case they should think she was losing her mind.

One day she was visited by her sister from Bristol, who brought with her a friend, Miss Roberts. Both women were concerned to find Mrs Keogh obviously distressed, but she still did not reveal what was troubling her; they were left with the impression that she was frightened of something. Miss Roberts offered to stay and keep her company for a few days, an offer which was very gladly accepted.

Miss Roberts had been in the house for three days, with nothing untoward happening, when Mrs Keogh went as usual to collect her son from school at 3.30 in the afternoon. Mrs Keogh returned to find her guest collapsed in the front room in a state of hysteria. Eventually Miss Roberts was able to tell her what had occurred. She said she suddenly heard footsteps coming down the stairs and turned to the doorway where the stairs descended to the living room, expecting the door to open; but it did not. She then felt the room go strangely cold. She was close to the sideboard smoking a cigarette, and to her horror became aware that the smoke from the cigarette, instead of spiralling up in the normal way, kept down to one level, *moving in a wavy line horizontally along the top of the sideboard.* She reached hurriedly for her coat, put it on and turned to the front door, but as she tried to open the door there was a sudden pressure on her shoulders like hands seeking to press her to the floor. She struggled up and again tried to open the door, but this time had the feeling of restraining hands round her ankles. At this she collapsed completely, slumping to the floor near the front door, which was how Mrs Keogh found her.

Miss Roberts went back to Bristol that same day.

The noises in Mrs Keogh's house continued all that summer and into the winter. One night after midnight, when they were particularly bad, she went in desperation to the public-house directly opposite and knocked up the licensee, telling him that there was "someone" in her house and she was afraid to stay in it. The licensee found a policeman and together they went to the house. The constable made a thorough search but found and heard nothing; yet as soon as Mrs Keogh was alone again the ominous knocking restarted.

Caught in a nightmare that seemed never-ending, Mrs Keogh was now forced to tell others about the ghostly noises, and found that her next-door neighbour, Mrs P. Butler, had also heard the sound of the chain on the bedroom mirror being rattled. Mrs Keogh finally sought the help of Birmingham psychical research workers, and a seance was held in the house. At this, in the presence of several witnesses, Mr A. T. Steadman, a medium from Solihull, made contact with the ghost, which said it was that of

Samuel Greatrex, a man who had lived in Mrs Keogh's house in the 1920s. Speaking through the medium, "Greatrex" said he had been jailed for a knifing incident in the house, and had died at Dudley Road Hospital after being transferred there from Winson Green Prison, where he was serving his sentence. At a second seance held shortly afterwards "Greatrex" repeated the information about himself, and at a third seance his "voice" coming through Mr Steadman was tape-recorded and pictures taken of the medium in trance. Again "Greatrex" talked of the stabbing incident in April, 1927.

Mr Steadman told me, "I saw him so clearly that I was able to make a sketch of him. He was wearing a white robe and carried a knife in his hand. He said he had hidden it in the pantry of the house."

In describing his arrest "Greatrex" gave the name of the police inspector who dealt with him, an Inspector Dixon. He said he was taken to Small Heath police station, and when he got there the police were having their sandwiches. He also mentioned two priests who visited him in hospital. The hospital and prison records were later checked and the ghost's information found to be perfectly correct, as were all the names given at the seance. In addition a retired policeman, PC James, was found who was on duty the night Greatrex was arrested, and who remembered the incident well.

Why had Greatrex haunted Mrs Keogh and not any of the previous tenants of the house in Garrison Lane? Because, the medium found, Greatrex was a Catholic, and as Mrs Keogh was a devout member of the same faith and furnished her home with religious ornaments, it was this which had brought him back. Through the medium "Greatrex" told Mrs Keogh, or "Kate" as he referred to her, that he was sorry for what he had done and would try not to bother her in future.

Mrs Keogh, however, left the haunted house and refused to go back. For three months she lived at a Corporation hostel, until another suitable house was found for her at Upper Thomas Street, Aston, a short distance from her former home. This was early in 1964—almost a year from the start of the hauntings.

Mrs Keogh's first day at her new house was peaceful, but on the second day, to her utter despair the familiar knockings and footsteps on the stairs began all over again. There was also on one occasion a loud bang from the storage cupboard, and on looking inside she found that her son's rocking horse, which she had put there, had for no reason been thrown to one side. Appalled, she sent for the medium, and a seance was held in her new home. After this the widow removed from the house all her religious ornaments except a single plaster statue. But still the knocking on the furniture continued.

A further seance was held, and at this Mrs Keogh herself broke in and appealed to "Greatrex", saying, "Why are you making my life a misery? Go away—why don't you leave me alone?" The ghost's reply through the medium was "I'm sorry, Kate, but I like the atmosphere here." The voice added, however, that it did not want to make her unhappy and promised not to be a nuisance.

But the promise did not hold good. The knockings continued intermittently; as, I am told by Mrs Keogh, they still do. But there are no more violent noises and Samuel Greatrex knocks unheeded, for she just isn't frightened of the ghost any more.

THE MONKS OF ST DUNSTAN'S

In East Acton, London, the spire of St Dunstan's rises in an area of sudden near-quiet reached surprisingly on turning out of the heavy traffic stream of Western Avenue. Built of dull red brick, the big church stands solid in its grassy and leafy square of ground in Friar's Place Lane, closely flanked by modern semi-detached houses. The footpath leading back from the pavement to the church door continues on to give access from one road to another, and the church's stained glass windows are protected by wire guards against the stones of young vandals.

The scene was vastly different in the 1870s, when the church was built. Then, not far away was the stately mansion of Friar's Place, which, with its magnificent grounds, hothouses and fountains, was one of the showplaces of Middlesex. The mansion fell into decay at the turn of the century and was demolished; now an ice-cream plant stands on the site, renamed The Friary. A persistent local tradition says that in the Middle Ages the old Friar's Place estate, on the edge of which St Dunstan's church stands, formerly belonged to St Bartholomew's, Smithfield, and that a "cell" or outpost of the St Bartholomew's friars existed there. If this tradition holds true, and it seems to be historically well supported, then there seems little doubt as to the identity of the phantom visitors to St Dunstan's.

The strange story of the haunting of St Dunstan's begins one Sunday morning early in the 1930s, when the then curate, the Rev Philip Boustead, was walking home with the assistant organist after the service. Mr Boustead, a much liked elderly priest who had taken holy orders late in life, had then been curate at St Dunstan's for many years, and on this Sunday morning his companion casually remarked on the history of the church. Mr

Boustead appeared to be lost in thought for a short time. Then he said, very earnestly and impulsively, "I must tell you something. I cannot tell anyone else, because they will laugh at me. There is something strange about our church. I have seen things when I've been alone in there. Some of these old monks who used to live round here. No, no—I don't want to say any more, but I know there is something there. Now please don't tell anyone else what I have been saying. They'll think I'm mad".

His surprised companion never did divulge this conversation; not until this account came to be written. But as will be seen later, Mr Boustead did confide in at least one other person.

A few years afterwards, in the winter of 1937-38, there came news of hauntings in the neighbourhood; not at St Dunstan's, but at the northern edge of the old Friar's Place estate, scarely more than half a mile away. Here, at the junction of Horn Lane and Western Avenue, an old world building which had preserved its ancient air in a changing neighbourhood, was said to be troubled by the spectre of a monk. This former farmhouse, which had become St Gabriel's Vicarage, with its cell-like cellars, cobbled paths, and what was thought to be the remains of a medieval courtyard, was then up for sale as it was too big for the vicar's needs. The vicar, the Rev C. V. Camplin-Cogan, though himself highly sceptical about the haunting, admitted that people who stayed in the house had heard uncanny noises, and that these were supposed to be caused by the ghost of an old monk buried under a cobbled path just outside the house. The vicar's wife said that she had often heard noises like padded footsteps on the stairs and in the hall, but on going to look had seen nothing. Then the apparition had appeared. A bedroom in one of the older parts of the house had a marble floor—it was thought to have been used as an oratory—and a startled guest who slept in the room described to the vicar and his wife how he had seen the shadowy figure of a monk suddenly appear in it. The harmless spirit, it seemed, had returned to wander about its former home.

The haunting of St Gabriel's Vicarage was looked upon as a fleeting wonder, more arguments being raised over the actual age of some old parts of the building rather than over the ghost, though it was generally agreed that if the monks of long ago had not actually lived on the vicarage site they had certainly lived close by to it, on the old St Bartholomew's land.

Six years later, in December, 1944 a new vicar came to St Dunstan's. The Rev Hugh Harold Anton-Stephens, who was in his fifties, had held two long ministries in Cheshire and London, and in his younger days had served as an Army chaplain. He was a widower, his wife having died only that year. Mr Anton-Stephens had not been many months at St Dunstan's before, like the late Mr Boustead, he found there was something very strange about the church; but he kept his own counsel about this, until one day he chanced to hear of the recent haunting of St Gabriel's Vicarage. After checking back carefully on the circumstances of this, he decided it was time to make public his own extraordinary findings at St Dunstan's, and accepted an invitiation to write an article for the local newspaper, the *Acton Gazette*. The article was published in November, 1946, and in it, after noting "the familiar attitude of respectable scepticism" at the time of the vicarage haunting, and recalling that the ghostly figure seen was that of a monk, Mr Anton-Stephens revealed:

"About a dozen such monks can be seen on most evenings walking in procession up the centre aisle and into the chancel of St Dunstan's church. They wear golden brown habits and are hooded. Another monk attired in eucharistic vestments occasionally celebrates Mass in the memorial chapel. Four of us, unknown to each other, have witnessed these phenomena, from time to time. We are all truthful folk and it is impossible for four people to suffer from the same hallucination at the same time.

"More interesting is a solitary monk, wearing a violet hood, with whom we hold conversation.

"The procession of monks probably belonged in some past age to a religious foundation in the locality. They are attracted to the nearest consecrated building. Their deepest satisfaction is to repeat what was their greatest happiness during earth-existence.

"My violet-hooded friend belongs to a different class. He is a ministering spirit, sent to inspire and instruct. I am indebted to him, as to many others, for much help." This monk, said the vicar, had recently given him advice regarding confirmation classes at the church.

Mr Anton-Stephens, after firmly establishing the appearance of the apparitions, went on to suggest in his article how such spirits could inspire, encourage and guide those who saw them. He invited debate on the subject. He was, I am told by a parishioner of the time, far more concerned with the religious aspect of the phenomena than the ghostly one. This parishioner, who was one of those who saw the monks prior to the vicar's disclosures, tells me, "I saw them three or four times on evenings when a discussion group was being held in the vestry. Because of the warm weather the vestry door leading into the body of the church was kept open, and I saw exactly the same thing on each occasion: a body of monks in brown habits walking in procession up the central aisle towards and into the chancel. Seen out of the corner of the eye they were clear, but disappeared when looked at directly.

"I knew nothing of any previous sightings or of the history of the church. The experience had no emotional impact on me—they were just monks walking up the aisle. When I mentioned the occurrence to the vicar he was quite matter of fact about it."

Not so the newspapers which immediately took up the vicar's story. They were intrigued by the unusual spectacle of twelve ghosts appearing together, and found from the vicar that those who had seen the manifestations included another parishioner who helped as his secretary.

As dusk set in on the cold and rainy November evening following Mr Anton-Stephens' disclosures, a reporter of the *Daily Graphic* made his way to St Dunstan's with the declared intention of either confirming or disproving the curious story. The vigil, however, produced more than he had bargained for.

The reporter, Kenneth Mason, wrote that he took a seat up in the far left-hand corner of the darkened nave. He was tired and cold, and wet; and the silence of the deserted church and the heaviness of the atmosphere combined to force him into sleep. It was with the thought of the monks that he closed his eyes. What it was that wakened him he did not know, but as his eyes opened he saw the phantom monks, six of them, in grey gowns, hooded, with heads bowed.

"Slowly but happily they came towards me. I took my courage in both hands and barred their way. I faced them. Then quickly I had to turn and look back at them. They had passed right through me."

The monks, who were walking to the altar, passed through Mr Mason two-by-two—"slightly below my neck and to the left of my collar bone". The time was ten minutes past seven. As they walked on he was aware of a voice speaking to him.

"'Near here, 500 years ago,' the quiet voice told me, 'stood a monastery. We were its occupants. This is our past, this is our future.' Reverently the monks genuflected to the altar. Then at the back of the church a light snapped on. A human voice spoke and the spell was broken. From the tower came the mournful toll of the service bell. As its sound the monks vanished, while I was left, uncomfortable, wide awake, wondering.

"That is all. I cannot explain it; that is not my function. But these things I saw last night."

A footnote to this surprising report in the newspaper stated: "Kenneth Mason is a quiet, sober-minded, reliable reporter who has never dabbled in the occult. He was a lieutenant in the Royal Navy during the war."

Mr Mason held his vigil on a Friday night. During the weekend he returned to St Dunstan's with a photographer, in the hope of obtaining a picture of the manifestations. By the vestry door, one of the twelve ghost monks, plainly visible to Mr Anton-Stephens, his secretary, and a parishioner, stood looking on as the camera-man tried vainly to snap him; but Mr Mason saw nothing. He reported, "The distraction of children trying to peer inside, and the babel of people wanting to see the ghost, upset the atmosphere of my previous vigil."

St Dunstan's now became an attraction for many curious sight-seers. The way in which the ghost monks had caught the popular imagination, to the exclusion of the more serious examination of such phenomena which he had tried to encourage, greatly disappointed the vicar. He wrote in the parish magazine a few weeks later:

"I was rather afraid that the popular Press would vulgarize the manifestations I described, but I was not prepared for the avalanche of letters which reached me from all parts of the world. Apparently every newspaper in the USA published a third-hand account. I was interested to hear from a former Sister here that the curate of her day (Mr Boustead) saw similar phenomena, and from the Psychic Research Society to the effect that they have had St Dunstan's monks on their records for over 12 years. They tell me that the manifestations occur in four-year cycles. As I suspected, more people have witnessed the phenomena than I knew."

The vicar continued: "May I repeat that, apart from the congregations, there are no spirits in the church. These visions are merely thought-pictures, televised by subtle rays, the nature of which are as yet unknown to scientists, but of course somewhere there is a personality responsible, consciously or unconsciously, for the vision. Please dissuade curious sightseers from visiting the church. The whole business is really very trivial and common-place, and was only mentioned as an introduction to the more serious matter of my original article. . . ."

And he added, just by the way: "You may be interested to know that the 'radiation' was almost overpowering during the midnight Eucharist." (Christmas, 1946).

The vicar declined to allow more vigils in the church and did not refer to the monks again publicly for many months. When at last he did so the result only added to his disappointment and annoyance. In the January 1948 parish magazine he told how he had been telephoned by a most friendly newspaperman "who asked if he might trespass on my valuable time for a chat. He came, and we talked for hours on the most fascinating subject of psychic phenomena, especially as related to religion and philosophy. At times we ascended into the heights of metaphysics and fourth dimensional thought, and both thoroughly enjoyed ourselves. . . ." The reporter was shown over the church, and, said the vicar, "I made one stipulation about anything he might write, and he willingly agreed. It was that the subject should be kept a sacred subject and not written about lightly or sensationally. Some of you saw last Wednesday's paper and know how horribly the promise was broken. Not one so-called fact is true. There was no owl in the churchyard, no hand on a doorknob, no conversation with the organist, no mention about a 'violet monk' in church last Sunday, no stumbling, and no command from me to be quiet. There was no wind and no strange noises. . . ."

In spite of this unfortunate experience Mr Anton-Stephens went ahead and published in the parish magazine some weeks later an article on confirmation headed "Supernatural", which he said had been dictated to him by the violet-hooded monk. It concerned the Te Deum and suggested how it might be altruistically expressed.

The vicar said he believed the violet-hooded figure to be the spirit of a monk who died in the ninth century. The monk had continued to appear and converse with him generally through the medium of his secretary, who conversed with the monk while he wrote down the conversations. The monk, who had promised other contributions when he had time to take them down, always appeared at confirmation classes. The other monks had made no verbal communication, though they had now been seen by a number of parishioners.

There were also many sceptics among the parishioners; yet there were further incidents that could not be explained. One of those extremely sceptical about the ghosts was Mr F. H. Harris, who as a churchwarden and, during staffing troubles, a sort of voluntary verger, was much about the church with no one else present. Mr Harris often said in a scoffing way that he had been locked up in the church alone hundreds of times, but the only noises he had heard were those of the pigeons pattering and fluttering about in the belfry. But very shortly before his death in 1948, he one day said to his wife, quite out of the blue, "You know, the vicar is right after all. There *is* something in that church—I've seen the monk." He also spoke of the incident to a local shopkeeper with whom he had been friendly for many years

There were other incidents. Mr R. N. G. Rowland, the St.

c

Dunstan's organist, tells me: "One Sunday evening after service, I was leaning over the back pew side-by-side with another chorister, discussing music (not a word or thought about ghosts), and we were staring vaguely down the church towards the chancel. The only others in the church were the vicar, the vorger and a warden, who were in the vicar's vestry. The nave was fairly well lit, the chancel in darkness. Quite suddenly, for no apparent reason, we stopped talking (we had been having an animated conversation) and stood silent gazing up into the chancel. I was aware of unseen activity there, and in a low voice said to my friend, 'Do you see anything?' He answered 'No, but there's something going on in the chancel.' I said, 'The vicar says that they hold services there.' 'Oh, the monks,' he replied. 'Yes, I believe it now. I didn't before, but I know they're there now.' "

On another occasion, with the vicar present, Mr Rowland was conducting choir practice with his assistant at the organ. "We were rehearsing Stanford's 'And I saw another angel' for All Saints' tide. In one of the more lush, full passages, looking a few bars ahead, I saw a typical 'horn cue' in the organ accompaniment. I said to myself, 'Oh, for an orchestra to do this full justice.' At that moment we reached the 'horn cue' and I distinctly heard the two horns—an effect quite impossible to reproduce on the organ—singing out their parts above everybody else. After we had finished the anthem I said to the vicar, 'Well, if it goes like that on Sunday, we shan't have anything to worry about.' 'Yes, very good,' he replied, 'but you might not have the orchestra with you on Sunday.' 'What orchestra?' I asked, deliberately. 'Come off it,' he said, 'you know as well as I do that you had a full spirit symphony orchestra out there in the chancel, playing along with you. Didn't you see them? I did.' 'No,' I replied, 'I did not see them.' 'Ah, but you knew they were there, didn't you?' he said. And somehow I could not deny it."

A former chorister tells me that Mr Anton-Stephens continued to take the church phenomena so much as a matter of course that in the years following, most of his parishioners became quite as cool about it all, the non-believers because of their distaste for the subject and the others because they were quite prepared to believe, from the vicar's casual statements made from time to time, that he did indeed "see ghosts". He explained the four-year cycle of the twelve monks very simply as a build-up of spirit-energy in the church over this period which then manifested itself in a fairly rapid series of appearances, and then lapsed to begin the build-up all over again. The violet-hooded monk, on the other hand, obeyed no definite cycle.

At all times during the remainder of his seventeen years' ministry at St Dunstan's the vicar was perfectly open about the church phenomena and the subject as a whole, whether joining in a discussion with the Over-21 Club and giving his views on the "spirit" causes and interpretation of some dreams, or by putting constant emphasis on spirit influences in life and on the ministry of angels. He did not, however, publish anything more ascribed to the violet-hooded monk, nor did he encourage further investigation of the church ghosts, because of the sensationalism which he so disliked. Retiring in 1961, he died shortly afterwards without publicly mentioning the subject again.

Do the monks of St Dunstan's still walk?

Mr Rowland, the organist, tells me of an incident late in 1966:

"I went into church one evening, about half an hour before the boys' choir practice, to play the organ. The church door was open to allow the boys to enter as they arrived. After playing for some ten minutes I felt a movement behind me, as if someone had stepped into the choir-stall and was standing behind my left shoulder. For a split second I assumed that one of the boys had arrived early, and I looked over my shoulder. There was no one to be seen—but there was certainly someone standing there. I had not stopped playing, and I just carried on, projecting a thought of 'Good evening—it's nice of you to come and listen to me.' I had no sense of fear or discomfort, rather a sense of elation. And until a boy came in a few minutes later, and broke the spell, I know that whoever was standing there was emanating a feeling of pleasure and approval, and wanting me to go on playing because he was enjoying it so much."

It was only the moment after setting down this account of the incident for me that Mr Rowland, to his own surprise, heard from a third party that two years earlier his son, an organ student, had had a similar experience when playing the organ alone in St Dunstan's.

"Avoiding leading questions, I asked my son about this at the next opportunity. He told me that on one occasion only, he sensed that someone was standing in the choir-stall immediately behind his left shoulder. However, not liking the experience he immediately switched on all the chancel lights—to that moment only the organ lights were on—and the feeling passed."

St Dunstan's, it would seem, might have its monks yet.

FOUR KNOCKS AND NO MORE

The King family moved into the Manor House, a typical old-fashioned farmhouse in Sussex, during the early autumn of 1933. In a few weeks they were happily installed in their new home, which stood in the charming hamlet of Denton, situated in a hollow of the Downs near Newhaven.

The house, which adjoined the churchyard and lay about 150 yards from the old rectory, was a sturdy building which had withstood the test of two centuries. A stone over the front door bore the inscription "P.M. Esq., 1724". It was a house of character, most of its fourteen rooms being reached by winding passages. One of its less attractive features was a dismal, dark and dungeon-like cellar, in which could be seen the doorway of a secret passage believed to lead under the churchyard to the church. This entrance, however, had long been bricked up, and the door of the cellar itself, reached through a room to the left of the front door, was kept bolted.

For the next seven weeks Mr and Mrs Sydney King, their twelve-year-old daughter, and Mr King's mother, Mrs Heasman, who was in her seventies, had perfect peace. Then, at intervals over about a week, Mrs Heasman heard strange, unaccountable noises in the house. Once there was such a loud bang from one room that she thought a wardrobe had fallen over, but on investigation this was found to be undisturbed.

The family were more puzzled than alarmed by these odd noises and it was not until a few days later, on a Sunday night in November, that the incident occurred which plunged them into terror.

On this night Mrs King was walking in a passageway leading to two bedrooms when she was suddenly confronted by a ghostly figure. Her shrieks brought her husband running to her. He grabbed a stick and beat at the apparition, but the stick only cut through it and struck the wall, breaking under the force. The ghost, which was of indeterminate appearance, melted away.

There then followed a series of terrifying thunderous knocks—one, two, three, four at a time. There were never more than four knocks and, repeated at intervals, they could be heard right through the house.

For the next three days the occupants of the Manor House were haunted by the eerie knocking, which played havoc with their nerves. It followed Mrs King to the scullery and other parts of the house to which she went alone, yet nearly always seemed to emanate from the centre of the house. The knocks seemed to follow a regular cycle, generally being heard at either twenty minutes to or twenty minutes after the hour, at intervals of five or six hours.

All the family heard the weird banging, as did two visitors to the house. Besides this, the cellar door started playing tricks, frequently being found open after it had been left firmly bolted.

The rector of Denton, the Rev E. Pinnix and his wife, were told of the ghost noises and on the Wednesday, with the family's nerves now stretched to breaking point, they stood in the house at different times and clearly heard the banging—one, two, three, four knocks at a time. Mrs Pinnix afterwards declared she would never forget the terrible shriek which they caused Mrs Heasman to give.

The rector offered a prayer in the house, in case the ghost should be an earthbound spirit in need of release. But it did little good, the noises continuing just as strongly as before.

Mr King decided that his family had suffered enough, and they packed up and left the house that night for a new home a quarter of a mile away. The empty Manor House was securely locked up but not abandoned, a policeman and several men keeping vigil outside. At about 10.20 pm. the stillness of the night was broken by the sound of heavy knocking coming loud and clear from inside—one, two, three, four knocks and no more. At once the front door was unlocked and the constable and his helpers rushed in with their torches, but though they searched the house thoroughly from roof to cellar, they found nothing.

One of the searchers had an unenviable experience. He said that while alone in a darkened room he distinctly heard a rustle as of someone rushing along the wall for about two yards. He immediately flashed his torch on the spot, but the room was empty.

Next day a reporter from the Brighton *Evening Argus* arrived to find the family packing up the last of their belongings for removal from the haunted house. He wrote in astonishment: "I heard the noises myself. I was standing in one of the rooms talking to the rector when suddenly, from the direction of the scullery, there came the sound of four distinct knockings, followed by a loud shriek from Mrs King, who had shortly before gone in that direction. She almost collapsed and had to be assisted into another room."

These knocks followed only forty minutes after identical bangings heard by the King family and two helpers. There was further evidence, too, of the peculiar behaviour of the cellar door. As the reporter entered the room, one of the visitors suddenly noticed that the cellar door was open again, though it had been securely bolted only a short time before.

The Kings now lost no time in vacating the premises for good.

What was behind the mysterious knocking? Many people locally were convinced that the haunting sprang from a former occupant of the house, long since dead, who had planted some trees in the front garden and declared that they should never be cut. They never had been until the previous Saturday—the day before Mrs King saw the apparition—when her husband cut them down.

When the disturbances at the house were revealed, two young girls who lived some distance from it told of a weird experience they had had one night three weeks earlier. They had gone out together to post some letters and when passing the old rectory heard a rustling in the trees. They turned to see a figure in white standing on the wall, and ran terrified from the spot. The apparition, they said, had no visible features; it was transparent and they could see right through it.

Whether this was the same nebulous figure which Mr King had tried ineffectually to beat off with his stick there was no means of confirming, but on the Saturday, at the end of the week of excitement, there came final proof from the Manor House of its noisy intruder. That night, in pitch darkness, as a knot of sightseers stood close together outside the padlocked gate of the old farmhouse, suddenly from inside the deserted building came a loud bang, followed by a second, a third and a fourth. Then silence.

It was the ghost's last fling.

The frightening bumps in the night that suddenly haunted a Lancashire family not long ago occurred in an ordinary terraced house, and were so loud that they could be heard at the end of the street, 200 yards away.

It was on Christmas Eve, 1959 that mysterious banging sounds began in the house in Tully Street, Salford, occupied by Mrs Clive Hill and her husband, and their twelve-year-old son. The noises started at about eleven o'clock, in the living room ceiling, and went on until 2 am.—"like an iron ball bounding on the ceiling". They continued over Christmas and into the New Year, hardly missing a night, resounding along and across the street, and disrupting the sleep of neighbours.

Mrs Hill and her husband searched under the floorboards and in the rafters for some physical explanation for the weird noises, but found nothing. To the house then came a procession of water board men, gas men, town hall officials and police, all of whom examined the premises thoroughly and left baffled.

Psychic research experts from Manchester University also searched the house and studied the noises. They were found to represent a code: one bump for "A", two for "B" and twenty-six for "Z". The bumps seemed to be spelling out messages to a neighbour, Mrs Freda Roberts, from her father-in-law, who had died some time ago, some of the later messages containing very personal things which only "Teddy", the father-in-law, could possibly have known. An investigator told the family that it seemed their son was being used by the spirit to communicate, for the boy remained quite oblivious to the noises at all times.

Further confirmation of the fantastic noises came from the Rev Edward Dimond, rector of St James's Church, Broughton, who came to the aid of the distressed family as the bumps continued for weeks on end, right through January and into February, 1960. Mr Dimond was sceptical when first told, but after hearing the noises himself on two nights he was convinced they came from something supernatural. No one, he said, could have made a noise quite like the persistent knocking, which was very loud and "just like a sledgehammer". He agreed that the spirit seemed to be answering questions by knocking a certain number of times to represent the letters of the alphabet.

Mr Dimond acted promptly. After consulting the Bishop of Manchester he decided to hold a special service in the house to drive the disturbing influence away. The twenty-five minute service was held on a night of February, 1960 while the Hills' son was upstairs in bed, Mr Dimond being assisted by a Manchester vicar. During the service police had to be sent for to move a crowd that collected in the street.

There was not a single noise after the service. The ghost seemed to have gone for good, and the thankful residents of Tully Street settled down once again to peaceful nights.

THE HEREFORD SENSATION

The first report of ghostly happenings in the ancient cathedral city of Hereford came, seasonably enough, just before Christmas 1932, when the news spread that two city policemen had encountered a phantom monk outside St Peter's Church.

It was shortly after midnight, the report went, when the two constables met in deserted St Peter's Square. At least, they had believed the square to be deserted, until one of them noticed a figure seated on or leaning against the War Memorial, wearing a long, dark, flowing robe. There had been a fancy dress dance that night so that the policeman promptly assumed that he had to deal with a stray reveller, and approached the man to ask him to move on. But as he got near to the robed figure it rose in silence and walked slowly towards the main porch of St Peter's Church, then, without pausing, melted through the massive iron gates of the outer porch, which were securely locked. As the other policeman hurried up to his astonished colleague, the monkish figure proceeded on its uncanny journey to the heavy oaken door of the church, also closed and locked, through which it vanished.

There could scarcely have been a more ideal setting for a ghostly visitation. St Peter's was built shortly after the Norman Conquest by Walter de Lacey as a priory for his monks, and its founder fell to his death from the battlements. Later, the provost of the little community of monks was murdered at the altar by the Welsh.

The present vicar, however, said he did not believe in ghosts and had never heard that his church was haunted, while the Hereford police proved very evasive and would not confirm the story.

This was a challenge to the *Hereford Times*, which determined to get to the bottom of the affair. The newspaper finally managed to question the policemen said to be involved in the incident, with the result that one of the officers denied having ever seen a ghost, but the other admitted that six years previously—in 1926—he and a constable no longer in Hereford had indeed seen the monk one night, exactly as had been described. Why had the incident only now come to light? Because, the newspaper discovered, a group of Hereford policemen had recently been discussing ghosts and the disclosure about the phantom of St Peter's was then made, and had leaked out in gossip.

It could all have ended there, a belated ghost story unsatisfactorily resolved, but as so often happens, corroboration came unexpectedly from another source. The son of the late Mr William Mason, who was organist at St Peter's for twenty-six years, revealed that his father claimed to have seen the spectral monk on a number of occasions. The first time, he saw the figure on the chancel steps, and, thinking it to be the verger, took no notice—until it suddenly disappeared. Two years later he again saw the figure, which he then described as "wearing a long dress, like a woman's".

Another time, said the son, his father told of seeing the same figure in the aisle. When he walked up to it, it vanished into the darkness. On yet another occasion he got quite close to the figure and saw clearly that it was garbed in a monastic robe. It walked noiselessly away and glided through the closed vestry door.

The son added that his father often confided to him that there was something uncanny about the church during the month of December, and in later years he would not go into the church alone after dark during that month.

In spite of these disclosures no investigation was made at St Peter's and the episode faded from the public mind. Two years later, however, the city was again the scene of ghostly activity, this time of much more sensational proportions; and oddly enough it was again two policemen who had first sight of the phantom.

The two officers, soon after midnight on an October night of 1934, saw a dark figure moving through the close of Hereford Cathedral. Because of its dark appearance one of the constables, mistaking it for a colleague, called out a greeting, at which the figure, which had been approaching him, immediately vanished. It was then realised that it had been wearing a cassock and cowl.

Not many days afterwards Mr W. E. Henner, a Hereford printer, also encountered the ghost. He was walking through the close at about 2.30 am. when he saw a sudden ray of light move across a corner of the Deanery, and when he had walked on a few more yards, another light quickly followed it. There was nothing to account for the strange lights and he was still puzzling over them when he saw a figure glide from behind a wall near the Deanery. Glued to the spot, he numbly registered every movement of the ghost. First the upper part of the body became visible, as if it were peering round the corner, then the whole figure appeared on the path, walking rigidly with hands at its sides. It was clothed in cowl and cassock of dirty white, but no face was visible. Mr Henner watched as it walked towards the Cathedral school and vanished behind the wall.

Only ten days after this, the ghostly monk was seen again by a young man returning to his rooms after walking his fiancée home. Mr S. H. Bach said he was passing through the close at about the same time, 2.30 am., when he saw the apparition, "swathed in a robe of dirty white and with its arms folded across the breast, gliding across the close with the air of one in deep contemplation".

These reports now decided a number of people to keep watch, and so on the night of Sunday, November 12 a party of eleven men and women made their way to the close to keep a vigil into the early hours. They took up their positions shortly after midnight and waited quietly opposite the cathedral entrance. At about two o'clock their patience was rewarded. According to all the witnesses, strange rays of light were seen to play upon one of the windows of the cathedral, then, within a few yards of them, there emerged from the wall on one side of the close the bent figure of a monk enveloped in cassock and cowl.

The watchers were perfectly ordinary people, not investigators, not experts, and not all believers in ghosts. What happened is described by one of them, Mrs Weaver, herself a sceptic until that night.

"I heard someone shout, 'Oh, there it is'. I turned round, and only a few yards away was the figure of a monk emerging, apparently, from the wall. It seemed to be crouching as if under a heavy load, and it walked silently across the close.

"I could see everything quite plainly—the cowl, and the dirty white robe with a lace fringe, covering a black garment. It stood out against the blackness of the night. I could not see any face. I was fascinated by the vision.

"I had heard that ghosts were troubled spirits, and, carried away by the desire to find out what was troubling the monk, I began walking towards it. I was not afraid of it then. As I walked, I recited the Lord's Prayer, and when I was within a few feet of the spectre I started to recite the Rosary. The figure of the monk vanished quite suddenly, and as it disappeared Miss Miles (another member of the party) pulled me away. The figure did not appear again."

Miss Violet Miles corroborated Mrs Weaver's story. She said the sudden appearance of the spectre gave her such a severe fright that she stumbled backwards, catching her leg on one of the chains that bordered the green. Her brother, Mr R. Miles, another member of the group and a decided sceptic, also testified to the strange scene, as did the rest of the eleven people, the younger ones among them not being fully recovered from the shock of their experience when interviewed the next day.

Excitement now ran high in the city and many people came to stare curiously in the close. They also came by night, alone and in crowds. One night, most of the passengers alighting in Hereford from a 2 am. train made for the close—"just as if they were going to a football match, there were so many on the same errand", one passenger said—while a noisy crowd of some 200 flocked there on another night in the hope of seeing the ghost. There was, in fact, such a constant traffic to the close, with some damage being done to the grass enclosures, that the clergy complained to the chief constable and the police took action to dampen the ardour of the ghost-hunters. The clergy did not accept that there was a ghost and maintained throughout that someone was playing a joke on the public. They were supported by others who suggested that the eleven people who together saw the ghost had been hoaxed by one of their members putting a handkerchief over his face and taking on the role of a spectre, though how he managed to make himself disappear into thin air was not explained.

With the police keeping a keen eye on visitors to the close the situation quietened, and the ghost itself made no further appearance during the next few days. But, just when all the excitement seemed to have died down there came another report of the monk being seen, this time in a different part of the cathedral grounds. Mr P. Thomas and his wife, Hereford residents, claimed to have seen the spectre near the library at the west end of the cathedral, some distance from the Deanery. First, they saw a strange light flash across a library window, and this was followed a second later by the ghost, a cowled figure walking slowly with its head down, as if looking for something or in deep contemplation. The startled couple were convinced that it was not a human figure and called to two soldiers, who came and also saw the monk before it vanished.

The controversy flared again, to be answered a few days later by the Dean, Dr Waterfield. In reply to suggestions that the monk might be trying to deliver a message, and that the clergy should keep a vigil and allow it an opportunity to speak, he said it was not likely that his clergy would "prowl about the close at midnight". Only that morning at two o'clock, the Dean added, "the 'ghost' was seen—but the person who saw it was in such an admirable position that it was possible to see that the figure was very much too solid for a ghost. It is obviously some hoaxer, and I am going to see the chief constable about it."

It seemed the last word on the subject, for after this the phantom figure was never seen again. But had the score of eye-witnesses all been mistaken? In spite of the Dean's conviction, many Hereford people remained unshaken in their belief that the thoughtful monk was a real ghost; and certainly nothing ever was found to prove them wrong.

LITTLE CHARLIE AND OTHERS

"I never believed in ghosts until these things happened to me and my family. I would have laughed if anyone had suggested to me before that a house could be haunted."

Time and again this same statement occurs in testimony given by eye-witnesses to police, clergy, reporters, investigators and others, and the strong feeling with which it is said can only be imagined. One who said it, in the summer of 1948, was the mother of two teenage boys, when describing their harrowing experience in the basement flat of a house in Swiss Cottage, London, which had been requisitioned during the war by Hampstead borough council.

The mother and her sons moved into the flat in 1946, and had been there only a short time when the uncanny incidents began.

Strange marks appeared on the doors and walls, and the mother began missing things. She thought her younger boy, aged fourteen, was responsible for this, and he was soundly spanked. But the incidents continued, knives and pokers mysteriously disappearing.

"One evening," she told the *Hampstead and Highgate Express*, "my curling irons vanished in front of my eyes. Six weeks later I saw them sticking out of the garden.

"Books flew in the air and landed on my son's head. None of our pets would live in the basement and had to be looked after by relatives.

"One night I came home and found my younger son hysterical with terror. He told me that hearing a noise in one of the cupboards, he opened the door and saw the figure of a crippled man standing before him. At first he thought it was a burglar and threw a milk bottle at the figure; but when the bottle passed right through and hit the wall, he rushed out into the street, where I found him sobbing his heart out.

"For months we endured lights being switched on and off, midnight tappings on the wall, and the room suddenly turning icy cold. One night I saw the ghost myself. It was so small and looked so ugly that I thought it was a monkey. I was even about to phone the Zoo and tell them that an animal had escaped, when the apparition vanished.

"I read up the history of the district to see if there was any reason for these manifestations. Then I called in some psychic research people and a number of seances were held in the flat. I learned that the house was haunted by an ugly hunchback murderer, and also a poltergeist."

The hunchback, apparently, had lived a hundred years ago, said the mother. At the seances she spoke to him and found that he was "very friendly." He told her he was sorry for his previous crimes and wanted to repent, and promised to leave the basement. She added, "We all call him 'Little Charlie.' He said that he murdered because of his ugliness."

Some further extraordinary evidence was now given by a woman who had lived in the flat from 1937 to 1939. There was definitely something strange about it, she said—"We used to find the lights being switched out or the curtains drawn, or even knives and scissors vanishing. We had no pets; they would not stay in the flat.

"I was cooking fried fish in the kitchen one evening when the room suddenly went cold. I turned for a moment to see if someone had opened the window. When I looked back at the stove the plate of fried fish had vanished. I never found it again."

The mother and her sons, when the haunting by "Little Charlie" was made public, were moved to a new council flat, though not on account of the ghost but "because of their domestic needs". The basement flat was renovated and let by the council to another tenant, when the hauntings by ghost and poltergeist apparently ceased.

The reactions of local authorities to complaints of ghosts are as unpredictable and varied as the hauntings that are so often brought to their notice.

In the same months as the Hampstead haunting, a family of five living in a flat in Bristol, suffered a haunting which kept them awake for sixty-three nights, and they finally had a recording made of the ghostly sounds, after which the city's assistant medical officer acted promptly to find the family other accommodation.

The noises that troubled Mr and Mrs J. Britton and their three children in their flat at Horsefair were mainly those of padding footsteps and eerie tappings; the only person who actually saw the ghost was Mrs Britton, who described the figure as that of a little old woman in brown with "a terribly evil face", whom she saw crossing the room towards her baby daughter's cot.

A psychic investigator was called in and a vigil was kept in the flat one night, with representatives of a sound recording firm standing by with their equipment. Just after 2 am. the sound of padding footsteps and irregular tapping began. Then suddenly Mrs Britton stood up rigid in the room, turned towards the cot and shrieked "My baby, my baby!" As a woman helping with the recording switched on the light and rushed into the room, Mrs Britton fainted and fell. She was unconscious for fifteen minutes, and on recovering said she had seen the apparition of the old woman come through the door and go towards the cot.

When the record was played over the noises and screams were reproduced, but there was also an unaccountable metallic vibration throughout the recording, which was one of the first to be made in a haunted house. The record was played over to Dr Irving Bell, the assistant medical officer, who said the noises seemed very genuine and he believed they might do harm to Mrs Britton's health, so he would look for other accommodation for the family.

There was no such swift help from authority for a young couple in Chorley, Lancashire, in 1954 whose little terraced house seemed plagued by ghostly footsteps, shrieks and scratchings, and the appearance of a grey figure. Mr Alan Mather and his wife had lived in the house since their marriage eighteen months before, and because they had decorated and furnished the house, in which they were tenants, they decided to say nothing about the manifestations but to try and put up with the grey, flitting shape, the size of a small man, which they both saw often in the house near the fireplace, and hearing the sounds of scratching, and a noise which they described "like a moan rising to a scream".

A priest blessed the house, but to no effect.

The climax came when the couple went out for an evening leaving the wife's eighteen-year-old sister sitting in with their ten-week-old baby. When they returned the frightened girl told them how, while reading, she had heard slow, deliberate footsteps overhead, and the footsteps then descended the stairs. The Mathers' dog, which was in the room with her, rushed to the stairs, but immediately turned round, its hairs bristling in fear, and hid under a chair. When Mr Mather went upstairs he found all the bedclothes had been thrown on to the floor.

It was the last straw, and the couple moved out to live temporarily with relations. There was no explanation for the haunting, and no record of previous ghostly activity in the house. The ghost did not deter desperate house hunters who sought the first chance to rent the property should the couple finally give it up.

There was no lack of prospective tenants, either, for a council house in Boston Spa, Yorkshire, which had been claimed by a succession of occupants to be haunted. In 1965 the housing committee of Wetherby rural council decided not to accept a vicar's offer to lay the ghost, or to act on letters that flooded in asking to be allowed to investigate the case, but simply to make repairs to the house to rectify a "peculiar smell", and then relet it for the fourth time in three years.

The three-bedroomed house, only fifty years old and modernised, was said to be haunted by the ghost of a young man dressed in tennis clothes and carrying a racket. One who thought his council colleagues had made the wrong decision was their Boston Spa member, Mr William Hill, who had had many complaints from successive tenants of the house. He said afterwards, "The last tenant was particularly disappointed. He was a young man who thought he couldn't be frightened, but after meeting the ghost in tennis kit he left the next day, saying 'Noises in the night are one thing, but meeting something face to face is totally different'."

The housing committee's view was put by its chairman, who said that if anything regarding a ghost needed to be done it was the tenant's job to organise it, not the council's. So after standing empty for three months, the house was let to a strong-minded young couple who said that as the ghost, if it existed, seemed not unfriendly, they should get along with it very well.

Birmingham Corporation in 1955 quickly received many hopeful applications for the tenancy of a house in the Ladywood district, which was vacated by a haunted family after only four weeks. In this instance, too, after some repairs the house was briskly relet, apparently without any resumption of the haunting. Yet the experience in the house of Mr Frank Pell, his wife and five children, is among the most strange.

The family, after having lived for two years in a condemned house, moved into the three-bedroomed house in Coxwell Road in June. It was newly decorated and a most comfortable home, and Mr Pell, an ex-paratrooper, and his wife had the house blessed for them by Father Francis Etherington, a local Catholic priest. But the hauntings began the weekend of their arrival. They were woken by the sound of banging doors, and there were loud thuddings on the kitchen ceiling at night which Mr Pell likened to blows from a twelve-pound hammer. There were also eerie whisperings and strange smells, like garlic, turning to the smell of burning rubber.

Three weeks after the Pells moved in, their month-old baby girl, who was sleeping with them, died during the night. At the inquest evidence was given that the baby, who was unmarked, had died from accidental suffocation, yet the parents, who on a hot night had thrown back the bedclothes, could not understand how the tragedy could have occurred.

The hauntings continued each night, with tapping on the ceiling above the kitchen, doors banging unaccountably, and the strange smells lingering in different parts of the house.

A few days after the baby's death, their four-year-old son asked his parents, "Did the baby go with the little white dog?" He then explained, "It comes and sits on my bed sometimes. I saw him sitting on baby's face the night baby left us."

The Pells had never had a dog.

Police searched the house and found nothing. Father Etherington, who came to hold a service in the house, stood with a relation in the upstairs room and heard the tappings and mysterious whisperings, which he afterwards described as like someone talking close to a microphone. The priest told Mr Pell that he had done all that was possible, and for the sake of their health the family should leave the house.

One morning Mr Pell was shaving downstairs when he heard the whispering again, just behind him. He knew that only his wife was in the house, and rushed to the stairs to see if it was her.

"She was standing at the top of the stairs, mouth open as if screaming, but I could hear no sound. I started to climb the stairs, then I stopped dead. There was some kind of invisible barrier I could not break. I caught hold of the banister and heaved. Suddenly I broke through. At once I could hear my wife's sobs and screams. She said the voices had been whispering to her as well."

The Pells resolutely quit the house and went to stay with relations living not far away. But still the strange tappings went on; two people who went to the house to collect some of the family's belongings heard them.

Council officials and workmen checked the house and found nothing wrong, and psychical research workers held a fruitless night's vigil in it. The family of eight to whom the house was then relet experienced no further trouble.

The Ladywood haunting had lasted only a month. A council-owned property in Dudley, Worcestershire, which became haunted shortly before the Pell's distressing experience, was all the more inexplicable because the family had been in occupation for nearly three years before the strange incidents began. The property itself was also vastly different. The Jolly Collier, at Holly Hall, Dudley, was a lonely century-old building at the bottom of a steep

D

bank in Low Town, which had been a public-house until shortly before the outbreak of World War II. It had since been converted as an ordinary house, though its nine rooms were still gas-lit.

After two peaceful years in the old building, Mr Edward Westwood and his wife and five grown-up sons and daughter heard strange noises for a period of some six months, but took little notice of them until shortly after Christmas, 1953 the various phenomena intensified and two apparitions suddenly appeared, one the figure of a young blonde woman wearing lipstick and other make-up, and the other that of a bald-headed man. The two ghosts appeared singly and in company.

The intense activity of the ghosts began, according to the family, when an eighteen-year-old son suddenly felt his bed move and was tipped on to the floor. He heard footsteps and uncanny knocking, but could see no one. He got back into bed and about half an hour later an alarm clock began ringing; yet there was no alarm clock in the house.

Then, footsteps were heard when there was no one about, and invisible hands touched shoulders and heads. Spiders' webs grew under water. There were shining lights at the windows, and the ghosts were seen often.

Mr Westwood called in the police, and while an officer was up-stairs investigating the room in which the blonde ghost first appeared, and which the family said was permeated with "the smell of death", the ghost of a young woman in a white shroud appeared at the window of a room below where Mrs Sarah Burton, sister-in-law of Mr Westwood, was sitting alone.

"The curtains parted and there she was," said Mrs Burton. "I screamed. I put my hands to my face and I was pulled from the chair by my hair. Before the policeman could reach me she disappeared through the window."

The almost daily ghostly incidents were too much for the family of eight, who in July, 1954 after reporting the strange happenings to the police, left the Jolly Collier to stay with neighbours.

The uncommon aspect of the lipsticked female ghost being seen in colour, when apparitions generally appear in monochrome, particularly interested psychical research investigators and two mediums, who kept night long vigils. The research investigators after a night at the inn came away without any evidence, but one medium said she contacted the blonde ghost who gave her name as "Martha", and appeared to have been involved in a murder.

The other woman medium, Mrs M. A. Brooks, from Birmingham, who investigated independently during two successive nights, claimed to have contacted both spectres while in trance. She said she saw the two phantoms emerge at the foot of the winding stair-case. "I saw them vividly, a man with a yellow dahlia and a peroxide-blonde young woman in a white and forget-me-not coloured blouse. There was also a child and another woman. I understood that among them there had been an illicit love affair."

Others sitting with Mrs Brooks in a downstairs room where a fire blazed, felt the temperature fall, and listened to the sounds of knocks and footsteps in the unoccupied room above.

Mrs Brooks and an assistant broke down two sealed doors and drained a stone well in the cellar in further unsuccessful efforts to clear up the mystery, as well as searching the dust-laden upstairs rooms.

For want of other accommodation, Mr and Mrs Westwood and four of their grown-up sons returned to the Jolly Collier, but, afraid to go into the haunted room upstairs, slept for a week together in the parlour, the parents in a double bed and the four sons huddled on the floor in the light of an old-fashioned fire. A week of further manifestations, during which they saw the ghostly blonde and her companion nearly every day, forced them again to leave and stay with a relative, but they had to return once more to the Jolly Collier, the whole family sleeping in one downstairs room, and Mr Westwood said that two of his sons lost their jobs through lack of sleep.

In the early months of 1954 the Westwoods had their second application to be rehoused rejected by the Dudley housing com-mittee. The Jolly Collier was considered suitable for the family and ghosts, said the committee chairman, were not a reasonable excuse for wanting to move house.

So the Westwoods had to continue living with the spectres of the old inn until the haunting subsided.

SIR GEOFFREY WALKS

The puzzle of why Geoffrey de Mandeville, the rebel Earl of
Essex, should return to walk the ancient parish of East Barnet,
Hertfordshire, is as intriguing as his phantom itself. For the earl
died in Suffolk and was buried in London, and as far as is known
he had not the slightest connection with East Barnet except that
at one time it formed a tiny part of his vast administration. Yet for
more than 800 years his ghost has been linked with the old village.

Strong-headed "Sir Geoffrey", as the earl is more popularly
remembered, played a dangerous game when Stephen and
Matilda were contesting for the crown of England, blatantly
taking honours from both. Pardoned in 1141 for treason against
King Stephen, he then became sheriff and justice of Hertfordshire,
and of London and Middlesex, as well as of Essex, wielding complete power over the capital and the three counties. He out-
matched all other nobles in wealth and importance and acted
everywhere as king; and was eagerly listened to. It was an in-
tolerable situation for Stephen, who, in 1143, having again the
ascendancy from Matilda and suspecting Sir Geoffrey of negotiat-
ing with her, sent officers to arrest him. The great earl, who was
attending his court at St Albans, was seized after a sharp struggle
and taken to London. There, under threat of being hanged, he was
made to surrender his strongholds in Essex and the Tower of
London, the principal sources of his might. He was then released.

But Geoffrey, though shorn of his more dangerous powers, was
by no means defeated. Bursting into open revolt he quickly set
himself up as master of the fenlands, forcing Stephen to march
against him. His inglorious death soon afterwards came as an anti-
climax, for the noble earl, while attacking a heavily fortified post,
carelessly removed his headpiece and was shot in the head by a
humble bowman. He lingered on for a few weeks before dying at

Mildenhall in September, 1144; excommunicated, because of his plunder of Church property, though he was later given absolution.

Such was the man, who, it was claimed, returned to haunt the old village of East Barnet. Through the years, tradition firmly linked his wraith with the village, while a further legend grew up that his ghost, clad in armour, red cloak and spurs, was also to be seen at Christmastime in Trent Park, Cockfosters, not very far away. This story, however, was bound up with hints of a hidden chest of gold, and told of outlawed Sir Geoffrey drowning in a well at Trent Park, which strayed a long way indeed from the historical facts. There might have been some confusion between two different apparitions, as does happen, but there was no doubting the link between Sir Geoffrey and East Barnet. And, not many years ago, there were dozens of people to testify that he walked the parish several times this century.

New prominence was given to the centuries-old haunting in 1925, when rumours spread of strange things being heard and seen at a stables at East Barnet, belonging to the local authority. It was the ghost of Sir Geoffrey, active once more, said those mindful of village tradition. The following year, the district council decided to pull down the stable and use its bricks in making a new road. Scarcely had this road work begun, however, than "Sir Geoffrey" was heard clanking his spurs as he walked across the floor of an old house in the locality. The same phenomenon was heard a second time in the house, and a third; while on another occasion, when it was again firmly established there could have been no human person about, there were impatient knocks at the front door and a rattling of the letter-box, which frightened the family and their dog. Odd noises were heard, too, near the road works, and finally a man walking past the haunted stables at midnight also heard the phantom spurs and, on looking round, caught a brief, startled glimpse of an apparition in a red cloak.

All this, occurring early in December, 1926 brought many reporters from London papers to the spot in search of a good ghost story, and a number of colourful reports of the East Barnet spectre, seemingly disturbed by the road works, were written but later denied, which served to make the whole affair highly suspect. Undaunted, a small group of interested local people gathered in the valley one night later on in the month to wait for the phantom and, according to their evidence, had a clear sight of the armoured earl in the moonlight. Because of the earlier events, however, their story was little believed and it was not until 1932, six years later, that the phantom of Sir Geoffrey was finally admitted to have been reliably and definitely seen by dozens of witnesses.

It came about through the efforts of a group of people actively interested in psychic matters, who, making careful inquiries in the East Barnet area, found that over the past twenty years, before which no records of any kind had been kept, the alleged visitations by the ghost had seemed to occur every sixth year—the last being the contested appearance in 1926. Older residents in the East Barnet valley said that at recurring intervals when the ghost appeared in the period between the full moon and the last quarter in the month of December, a strange, uncanny disturbance of the atmosphere developed as midnight approached. Acting on this information the group decided to hold a vigil, which was arranged for the night of Saturday, December 17, 1932.

In a freshening wind the group took up their position in the valley. They had waited patiently for some time when, just before the rising of the moon, they heard an uncanny noise like the clanking of spurs. It sounded first in the distance, and a moment later was heard around them at close quarters. The noise was repeated again and again, then became fainter. The watchers started walking slowly towards the fading sounds, making their way southward along the valley from East Barnet village on to land at Oak Hill recently acquired for an open space by the district council. And here their cold vigil was rewarded. On rising ground towards the east, with a woodland copse as a background, a sudden break in the clouds enabled the astonished group to see very distinctly in the faint moonlight the phantom of Sir Geoffrey, accoutred in his old-time armour. Their report of the incident stated, "The glance was a fleeting one, but very distinct, and the sight is fixed in the minds of those who saw it as plainly as if it had been revealed in midday sunlight".

The success of this vigil produced a great deal of excitement and hopes were high that the phenomenon would repeat itself on the following Tuesday night, St Thomas's Eve (the vigil of St Thomas, the apostle who doubted the existence of the spirit state) or on Christmas Eve, both days being especially favourable for ghostly manifestations. It was eventually decided to hold a second vigil on the Christmas Eve, and a general invitation was extended to anyone seriously interested to come along on that night and keep watch for themselves.

An hour before midnight on the Christmas Eve a crowd of curious sightseers gathered at the junction of Brookside and Cat Hill, at East Barnet. They drifted off in various directions while the group of investigators and others moved on a quarter of a mile southwards from the village to take up their position beside a small wooden bridge spanning the stream known as Pymms Brook. The bridge allowed wayfarers using the old church path to cross over on their way to Cockfosters.

As midnight approached this main group became aware of unusual sounds coming from the south. The sounds produced an uncanny feeling among them and they walked slowly on to investigate. After following the line of the stream through the recreation ground, they paused for a moment opposite Oak Hill, but all was quiet again. Continuing on in the direction of the cemetery they again paused opposite the locality of Monk Frith, when suddenly a long-drawn, wailing howl of distress was heard. As they stood and listened, highly tensed, the sound was repeated *among* the watchers. The night was very dark but they did not use their torches in case the spell should be broken. Then they heard, intermingled with this soulful howl of a dog, the clanking of armour. In a few moments they were conscious of movement and quite suddenly saw the shadowy form of a long-legged, headless hound slowly fading into the rising mist; without doubt, they thought, the phantom dog which legend had said often accompanied Sir Geoffrey, but which had not been seen by anyone within living memory. Next moment the clanking noise of armour seemed to surround the group, and they then saw the phantom of Sir Geoffrey clearly revealed. It vanished again into the mist as they watched.

The group made a detailed report of the incident which was placed on record with a psychic research society. There was, however, great disappointment and not a little scepticism among the many other people who had waited at other points in the valley and seen and heard little or nothing. But among those who had stayed close to the research group and could confirm what they had seen was a reporter of the *Sunday Dispatch*. Noting how some ghosts were most obliging, Sir Geoffrey appearing promptly on schedule, he wrote, "I, with many others, gathered in the old village to await the arrival of the ghostly visitor. The night was cold and cloudy. There was a woodland copse in the background. As we stood, staring, there was a sudden break in the clouds and there could be seen clearly a figure in armour—Sir Geoffrey de Mandeville.

"I made careful inquiries in East Barnet and found at least a dozen people willing to testify that they have seen the same phenomenon three times in the last twenty years."

Whether Sir Geoffrey appeared on the next of the six-yearly cycles we do not know, as there are no authentic records; understandably, as war was imminent and minds were on other things, while at the next cycle, war was in progress. So the phantom earl lapsed again into history.

Whether he continues his periodic return to modern East Barnet remains to be confirmed. Though the old village has seen the spread of red-bricked housing, its ancient history perpetuated only in the names of such pleasant residential roads as Monkfrith Way and Friars Walk, the open space of Oak Hill exists much as it was yesterday. And in the little valley, the December mists still gather.

THE MURDER STONE

Towards the end of the summer of 1821 Margaret Williams, an attractive Carmarthen girl, went into service at a small farm near the village of Cadoxton, in the neighbouring county of Glamorganshire, South Wales. She was a level-headed girl in her twenties, a hard worker whose industry and cheerfulness soon made her well liked in the district. Her charms also quickly registered with the farmer's son, and in time the two came to be seen together often.

It then became evident that their association was not faring too well and that the girl was troubled; but she asked no one's help and settled matters herself, giving notice to the farmer and leaving to care for an old man who occupied a small house not far away, near Neath. Here again her capacity for hard work was quickly noticed and approved by the neighbours, together with the cheerfulness she had now regained; but in this new community she made no secret of the fact that the farmer's son had made her pregnant. She was heard frequently to declare the wrong he had done her, openly giving his name.

Margaret Williams began her new job with her kindly old employer in May, 1822. Ten weeks later, on the morning of Sunday, July 14 her pathetically beaten body was found in a ditch on the marsh adjoining the village of Cadoxton. There was only sixteen inches of water in the ditch and though she lay on her left side with her head submerged, the ditch was too narrow to allow the rest of her body to sink into it. Both her arms were bruised, as well as her throat and neck, and clearly her attacker had used considerable force to overcome and strangle her.

Near her on the marsh lay the basket she had carried, containing her hat and a sheep's head which she had bought at Neath on the Saturday night.

The brutal murder aroused the intense anger of the entire district, all eyes looking in a certain direction for the killer. An inquest attended by several magistrates and landed gentlemen was opened on the Tuesday morning, and no sooner had the doctors confirmed that the girl had been violently attacked and strangled, and that she had indeed been pregnant, than a warrant was issued for the arrest of the farmer's son. He was taken at once and held prisoner to await the inquest verdict.

For two days the inquest went on, the jury themselves being locked up together on the Tuesday during the necessary overnight adjournment; but although the strongest suspicions existed against the prisoner, in all the evidence threshed out by the coroner there was nothing to establish the young man's guilt. The verdict of the jury therefore had to be one of "wilful murder by some person or persons unknown", and the suspect was discharged.

The deep feelings of the local people, which had been roused further by the heart-breaking scene when the girl's parents, summoned from Carmarthenshire, identified their murdered child, were well mirrored by *The Cambrian* which reported, "The magistrates have declared their resolution to seek out fresh evidence with unremitting scrutiny, and it is devoutly to be wished that the inhuman monster who perpetrated this foul and horrid deed may yet be brought to justice. The eye of Providence is upon him, and we trust the hand of Providence also will be with those who endeavour to find the clue of the discovery, which human wickedness and cunning have for the present concealed."

The strenuous inquiries, both official and unofficial, went on for months, but in spite of all these efforts the servant girl's killer remained at large. There was, however, little doubt that, as *The Cambrian* forcefully put it, "the unfortunate girl was murdered in a moment of confiding affection by a monster—rather a demon—in the form of a man, by whom she had become pregnant". The villagers were incensed by what they considered to be the escape of a callous murderer, and the local gentry no less. It was decided to punish him in the only way open to them, by striking at his conscience.

One of the local gentlemen, Mr George Tennant of Cadoxton Lodge, undertook to foot the entire expense of a memorial to Margaret Williams to be put up in Cadoxton churchyard. This was to be "a massive stone, extremely simple but of conspicuous form and dimensions", and Elijah Waring, brother of Letitia Waring, the hymn writer, was asked to compose an inscription for it which would convey the feeling of the community.

The "Murder Stone" was set up in Cadoxton churchyard on an April day in 1823, nine months after the discovery of the girl's body. For many Sundays afterwards people from miles around walked to the churchyard to see the ominous memorial, and those who could to read the damning inscription. This is what Elijah Waring wrote, as it appeared on the stone:

1823
To record
MURDER
This stone was erected
over the Body
of
MARGARET WILLIAMS
Aged 26
A native of Carmarthenshire
Living in service in this parish
who was found dead
With marks of violence upon her person
In a ditch on the Marsh
Below this Church Yard
on the Morning
of Sunday the fourteenth of July
1822

Although
THE SAVAGE MURDERER
Escape for a season the detection of man
Yet
GOD HATH SET HIS MARK UPON HIM
Either for Time or Eternity
and
THE CRY OF BLOOD
Will assuredly pursue him
To a certain and terrible, but righteous
JUDGMENT.
Canys nyni a adwaenom y neb a ddywedodd, MYFI
BIAU DIAL, MYFI A DALAF, MEDD YR ARGLWYDD
Hebreiad x.30

It was too much for the farmer's son, who vanished from the community and then from the country, never to be seen again. In after years the stone became the focal point of eerie ghost stories, and in winter, when night fell early and the wind whipped across the marsh and the churchyard, many people were afraid to pass by it. Several villagers swore they had seen two ghostly figures gliding near the stone, and it was firmly believed that these apparitions were those of the murdered girl and her lover, returned to the memorial which cried out for her revenge.

Stories of the ghosts being seen continued right up to the 1920s, a hundred years after the tragedy, when it was suggested that the stone, an embarrassing reminder of community hate, should be removed. The arguments for and against this went on for a number of years, but no direct request was made to the church for the stone's removal and so it remained in its position in the churchyard, near and facing the main road; and it is there still.

Though there have been no recent reports of the gliding ghosts, the cry of the outraged populace still seems to echo from the grim monument, ever strong.

Violence provides the background to many ghosts, and few hauntings are so weird as that following a murder in the Forest of Dean, Gloucestershire, in about the year 1840.

It became noticed that there was missing from the neighbourhood of Ruardean Hill a stonemason known by the nickname of "Get-it-to-go." He was last seen at a drinking-house and there was a whispered report of a quarrel and some blows being struck. It was thought that the stonemason had received what the foresters called "an unlucky blow"—and there were no police around to investigate.

Twelve months afterwards word got about that a strange ghostly noise was to be heard coming from the depths of a disused pit. A family living in a cabin nearby said the noise sounded like a man boring a hole with a hammer and drill. Rumour spread, quickly connecting the ghostly sound with the stonemason's disappearance, and the parish constables were ordered to make a search. A windlass was put up and the pit examined, but no body was found. The eerie noise, however, continued at intervals, until about a year later it was so loud and insistent that another wheel was put up and a second search made; and this time, when the bottom of the pit was cleared of debris, the searchers found the stonemason's body, or what was left of it after the attention of the rats.

A large crowd collected at the pithead as the body was brought up. The clothes helped to keep the remains together as they were shovelled into a coffin, which was afterwards laid down in the open for all to see. Timothy Mountjoy, from whose eye-witness account this record is taken, noted, "The wonder was that scores did not die from the horrid stench; it was reported that one person died from blood-poison."

Why was the body not found on the first search? Because, it was strongly believed, some of the men employed then to search the pit were those who had thrown the stonemason into it. On the discovery of the body the ghostly noise from the old pit ceased.

A particularly shocking accident was believed to be the reason for a macabre haunting of the railway track running through the little colliery village of Burnopfield, Durham, during the autumn of 1932. Here is the account of one man who encountered the ghost:

"I was coming down beside the line to get to Burnopfield, when I was stopped by hearing several metallic clangs, just like those a platelayer makes when laying or repairing rails. After stopping for a few moments I walked on, but my progress was again arrested by seeing a face hanging in mid-air. It was horribly twisted and scarred, and the eyes blazed in a terrible and eerie way.

"I saw the face for a second, then I heard a thunderous roar like hundreds of coal wagons out of control on the line. I did not stop for any more but turned and ran."

Several other people claimed to see on different occasions the twisted face, its head covered with a shock of white hair, and always the ghost's appearance on the colliery wagon-way was heralded by a number of clangs like a sledgehammer striking metal. Older people in the village recalled a distressing accident in 1879, when a platelayer on the railway was killed when the wire rope connecting a line of moving coal wagons suddenly parted. It seemed that the unfortunate man's agonised spirit had returned for a time to haunt the spot.

At Lydney Docks, on the River Severn in Gloucestershire, a man hanged for murder in the last century was thought responsible for a persistent haunting in the neighbourhood of the mortuary. At intervals through the years following his execution the ghostly figure of the murderer, who killed a woman on the marshes, was seen, though not too much notice was taken of the witnesses' stories. Then, in the autumn of 1934, a quick succession of incidents seemed to offer conclusive proof of the ghost's existence.

Among the first to report its appearance was a terrified young girl who said she was walking up the lock bank one night when something seemed to appear out of nothing in front of her. "Then I could see the misty outline of a man with a slouch hat and raincoat. I could not see his legs. I was terribly frightened and took to my heels and ran away as fast as I could. I am sure it was not a human being."

Another Lydney resident testified, "I knew nothing of the 'ghost' before I went down to the lock one evening. When I rounded a corner I was surprised to see something in front of me. It appeared to be a very tall man. I said 'Good night' but there was no reply and the figure vanished before I went further."

If there was still doubt that the raincoated figure was really that of a ghost, the frightening experience one night of another man seemed enough to dispel it. He stated, "I was riding my bicycle when suddenly, near the mortuary, I saw a figure surrounded by a halo of mist in front of me. I rang my bell because I thought it was a man. The figure did not move an inch, and I kept on ringing my bell. Just as I was about to jump off my machine to avoid a collision the figure vanished—just evaporated into nothing."

Other people, men and women, reported seeing the ghost, which always took the form of a light raincoated figure in a slouch hat, its legs not visible, standing immobile in the half light. All the witnesses vowed that when disturbed, it dissolved into thin-air. One old sailor admitted that he had seen the figure on several occasions over the past twenty years; it never made any sound, he said, and seemed just to stand or hover for some moments, gazing at passers-by.

Following this most recent spate of appearances by the ghost several attempts were made to lay it, but all the vigils were un-rewarded.

Murder was also thought to be behind a haunting at St Mary's Barracks, Chatham, the Navy's oldest barracks, though in this case it was the ghost of the victim that seemed to have returned. Unrest at the barracks, then in use as a naval gunnery school, became public in the spring of 1946, when young naval ratings protested at having to do sentry duty on their own at dead of night. They said that during the middle watch from midnight to four o'clock, while patrolling a long stretch of ramparts overlooking an old moat, they had heard, individually, mysterious footsteps padding along behind, and an incessant tap, tap, as of somebody walking with the aid of a stick. So alarmed was one rating that he ran off to the guardroom in a panic, the mysterious footsteps following him until he was off the ramparts.

It was on a night shortly after this that a startled rating, by the light of the moon, saw to his horror the figure of a man dressed in the uniform of Nelson's days, hobbling along the ramparts on a crutch. The man wore his hair in a pigtail as was then the fashion. The apparition eventually vanished into the moat which was twenty feet deep.

The rating, scarcely able to believe his eyes, reported the inci-dent to the guardroom and it was entered in the logbook: "Ghost reported seen by sentry during the middle watch."

The barracks, built in 1787 by French prisoners-of-war and convict labour, was honeycombed by underground passages and an official theory now put forward was that when the wind was blowing in a certain direction, footsteps reverberated through the passages beneath the ramparts, producing an echo immediately behind the rating on lone patrol. It was suggested that on hearing such "footsteps", the ghost-seeing sentry may have mistaken a bush moving in the wind for the figure.

Only two years later, however, the ghost of St Mary's seemed to return again. In Room 34 of the Cumberland block strange things began happening: sudden gusts of hot and cold air, unaccountable footsteps, chairs moving, and blankets being tugged from beds. Petty Officer Mechanic Joseph Dickson, of Newcastle, was told about these things by his four room-mates on returning from Christmas leave in 1948. He scoffed; but his scepticism received a sudden jolt when some days later he was roused from sleep at 2 am. by a mysterious jerk at his bedclothes. Three days later the same thing happened, and on both occasions everyone in the room with him was asleep.

The following day Dickson's colleagues went on leave, leaving him alone in the room. Now the ghostly incidents became more pronounced. He testified, "Again I felt someone touch me. I sat up and heard footsteps, as though whatever it was was wearing great nails in its boots. I put on the light, still hearing the footsteps, and searched the room, but there was no one there. I went back to bed and was just going off to sleep again when I heard the sound of someone poking the fire in the next room. I got up and went to the room, but it was empty. Then, perfectly clearly, I heard someone coughing in the room and I knew no living person was there."

It was what occurred the following night that finally convinced him of the ghost. Awakened by a cold draught of air, he sat up in bed to see the wardrobe door swing open before him. He got up and closed the door and tried to make it swing open by shaking it, but found that he could not. As soon as he got back into bed, however, the door swung open again; and then a chair moved about three feet across the floor.

Though the ghost was not actually seen on these occasions it was thought to be the same spirit as had haunted the ramparts two years before, and was commonly believed to be that of a sentry murdered by escaping French prisoners during the Napoleonic wars. The sentry's relief had been late and he was apparently following a ghostly errand to Room 34 to shake the relief from bed.

The old Royal Marine Barracks at Chatham, which were even older than St Mary's, also had their ghost officially logged not many years ago. Over a long period several Marines had reported seeing the ghost, which was believed to be that of a Marine who shot himself. When, after 167 years at Chatham, the Royal Marines left the barracks and the town in 1950, it might be thought that the ghost, too, would vacate the premises, but this was not to be.

Four years later, in 1954, the Naval Patrol which policed the streets of Chatham had made its headquarters in the former guardroom section of the otherwise deserted barracks in Dock Road. The area was fenced off from the rest of the barracks. At 6.30 one November evening, Leading Patrolman David Fell, a sturdy, level-headed man and among the biggest and heaviest members of the patrol, went up to his locker in a top-storey room to get some tobacco. The room, which overlooked the graveyard of St Mary's Church, was empty but for a few lockers and lit by a single 100-watt bulb. Suddenly out of the corner of his eye, Fell saw what appeared to be a solid figure standing near one of the windows. He swung round and the figure vanished before he could make out any details of its dress or appearance. Badly shaken he rushed down two gloomy flights of stairs to the patrol-room and told his incredible story. Even the strongest sceptics were impressed by his belief in what he had seen. The Master-at-Arms confirmed, "He is one of the best lads to have around in a tight corner and is not easily disturbed, but there was no doubt when he came rushing down here something had given him a really bad shaking."

No amount of ragging by other members of the patrol or official questioning by his superiors shook Leading Patrolman Fell's belief that he had seen a ghost, and the Provost Marshal was convinced of the reality of his experience. Accordingly a report on the incident went through official channels and finally reached the Commander-in-Chief Nore. Inquiries then made among Royal Marines formerly stationed at Chatham disclosed that this section of the barracks had reputedly been haunted for years by the ghost of a Marine who killed himself in the room now containing the lockers. Many times a mystery figure had been reported in this same room or nearby; and so strong had been the feeling about the supposed hauntings that one well known sergeant major had flatly refused to go near the room unless it was absolutely unavoidable.

The ghost's brief appearance in 1954 was the last recorded before the barracks was demolished a few years later.

The Congress Hall in Clapton, East London, used for fifty years as the training school for Salvation Army officers, would seem an unlikely place for a haunting resulting from sudden death, but a ghost walked there and was seen by many. The Army trainees called her "Maria" and she was still walking in the hall in the 1930s.

Maria was a nurse when the Congress Hall was a home for

foundlings in the last century. She murdered her own baby, hiding the body in a dark nook occupied in later years by the baker's oven; and, bitter-faced, she returned after her own death to pace the corridors.

A woman major just before the outbreak of World War II told how, when she was a cadet at the training school, Maria was frequently seen on a regular "walk".

"She went from the kitchens along the downstairs corridor, up the front stairs and past what we used to call Scotch Corner. I used to have to conduct a prayer meeting there when I was in training, and once I'm sure, if I had opened my eyes, I would have seen her. I did not dare look that time. But I have personal friends who swear they have seen her. She wears a grey nurse's uniform and does not look misty and ghostlike. One of my friends was reading in the library when we were cadets, and looked up to see Maria sitting opposite her. The ghost then just faded away."

Maria ceased her travels as war began.

THE HAUNTED HOSTEL

The early wartime case of the haunted hostel for girls really began for Miss G. Methvea Brownlee, a well known photographer in the West Country, when a bomb fell on her home in Charlotte Street, Bristol, on a November evening in 1940. In her own words, "That bomb destroyed all I had, and I felt that my one salvation would be to find a job."

She found one at Oldbury House, St Michael's Hill, Bristol, which the BBC had taken over as a hostel for girls on the staff. It was a very old house, reputed to have been used by Prince Rupert as his headquarters when Bristol was besieged in the days of Cromwell. Underground tunnels were believed to run from the house to the centre of the city, and to the old Bristol Fort.

Miss Brownlee's job was to look after the general well-being of the BBC girls. There were twenty-eight of them, all in their late teens and twenties, and there was a hostel staff of seven.

Miss Brownlee and her charges soon found that the old house also had seven other "residents". This is how she described the eerie experiences of herself and some of the girls soon afterwards.

"I slept on the ground floor by the front door, and was awakened frequently by thuds, by heavy dragging sounds, and by the sobbing of a child. Then, I saw the ghosts.

"There was a very tall, thin man, dressed like a monk, in long dark robes, with a bunch of keys hanging from a girdle at his waist. There was also a little old woman, dressed rather like a housekeeper of the same period; and finally there were five ladies, always together, dressed alike in clinging robes with high head-dresses.

"I discovered that there had been at one time an opening from my room to the stables beyond. It was here that I first saw the monk. After that, at frequent intervals, I saw not only the monk but the housekeeper also, and the five women together. The women seemed to stand on a balcony, as if in a vision. They talked agitatedly among themselves, and in the background there was the monk again, seemingly pleading for something.

"I said nothing about this to the girls as I did not think it would be good to arouse their imaginations. But one day several girls came to me and told me of things they had seen. Their experiences corresponded exactly with my own. Eight girls saw these presences in the house exactly as I did. The other twenty experienced nothing at all.

"Often two or three of the girls saw the figures simultaneously. On other occasions one girl would see a figure coming through the door, and a minute or so later another girl would see it at the end of the passage, and later still yet another girl would see it at the foot of the stairs."

In the space of three months the persistent hauntings so got on everyone's nerves that in March, 1941 the girls were moved away and the hostel closed. After that no one stayed overnight at Oldbury House, which was taken over by a Ministry and afterwards became the Bristol Inland Revenue tax office.

Seven ghosts together were also claimed to be seen in the late 1940s at Rye, Sussex, only in this case all of them were monks. Several people testified to seeing the phantoms at the Monastery Hall, a fourteenth-century Augustine Friars' chapel, walking in single file across the garden and through a ten-foot high brick wall.

Disclosure of the hauntings early in 1950 brought many sightseers to the chapel. The caretaker there, Mr Fred Parris, had become convinced some years before that it was haunted, but had said nothing so as to avoid publicity. He now admitted:

"I have seen the ghost of a cowled monk several times. He is tall, over six feet, and can walk through walls.

"Once, when I went to open the garden gate I stretched out my arm and it went cold and stiff, as if suddenly frozen. Then a few feet away I saw the monk looking at me. Another time I was chopping wood, when suddenly I began to grow colder and colder, and could not stop shivering. Then something tapped my head three times, and the coldness vanished."

Even indoors, said Mr Parris, he and his wife had felt a breath of cold air as if someone was walking through the room. No pets would stay with them. "We have had dogs, but they ran away or seemed to go mad. We have tried cats, but they became crazed and aged. We no longer keep pets." All the ghostly events, he said, occurred not at midnight but between tea time and dusk.

Part of the monastery's garden was excavated during World War II for an air-raid shelter, and a few feet underground a row of skeletons was discovered, all but one standing upright, and the other kneeling. Experts said the bodies had been buried alive. Mr Parris himself found skeletons in other parts of the garden.

One of the local theories for the haunting was that the monks of long ago resented the Monastery Hall now being used for entertainments, auctions and public meetings.

Among other cases of monks of the past returning to haunt their former homes, the incidents on Caldy Island in the 1920s are somewhat unique; for on this tiny island off the coast of Pembrokeshire, a spectral monk appeared among a community of monks still very active there.

The island, with its monastery and white-robed Benedictine monks, its Celtic church and twelfth-century priory, was owned by the Benedictines; there were thirty-six of them among the island's total population of ninety-eight. It was an almost self-supporting community, with no public-houses, no policeman, and no rates; and in complete silence the monks went about their tasks of praying and ploughing, spinning and weaving.

During the day the only sounds that broke the stillness were the lappings of the waves and the occasional chimes from the monastery tower; but sometimes at night the peace of the little "island of saints" was, according to the islanders, disturbed by ghostly shrieks, and villagers saw a ghostly figure. Some felt "something" brush them, while others spoke of an uncanny presence.

A strange black-robed monk more than six feet tall, with cowl drawn over his head, was reputed to wander round the ancient priory. It was said that his wraith rose from the burial ground, where monks had been laid to rest since the fifth century. On one occasion, after a dinner at the monastery, a woman who had been helping with the cooking found her path barred by the black monk. She turned and fled.

Several other of the islanders, who were given to no special flights of imagination regarding the monks with whom they lived daily, told of their encounters with the eerie black monk. One was Mrs McHardy, wife of the island bailiff, who said, "One evening, at dusk, I was sitting in our parlour at the old Priory Farm when I heard footsteps descending the stairs, and, going into the hall, I saw it was my son Jo. Then I shrieked, for behind him on the stairs I saw the gaunt figure of a monk in black robes with a face like death—grey and pallid—peering from beneath his cowl.

"As I gazed, the spectre faded and disappeared."

Mrs Stiles, another of the islanders, told how when she was walking down a lane one evening she came upon a ghostly black figure sitting or leaning on a fence. She could not see its face but said it was wearing a hat "like a mushroom". She took to her heels.

A white lady, and the ghost of a madman who buried himself alive were also said to have haunted the island in the past. There was a belief, too, that an enormous sapphire of great value, thought to have been brought to the island from Glastonbury Abbey at the dissolution of the monasteries, was hidden in the walls of the priory; at times what some islanders described as "a pointing hand" and others as a "luminous glow" was claimed to be seen on the walls, indicating, as it were, the position of the hidden treasure.

But in 1927 it was the intensified haunting by the black monk that worried the lay population. The Benedictines, who had then been on the island for some twenty years, made no comment on the apparition, which, oddly enough, seemed to end its startling appearances two years later, when the Benedictines left the island for Gloucestershire. Monks of the Cistercian order then took over Caldy's hillside monastery, continuing the silent work of their predecessors in the island's floral valley; and the black spectre was seen no more.

A less alarming sight than the Caldy Island spectre, and in fact an eagerly looked for visitation, were the five phantom monks or friars claimed to have appeared at regular intervals through very many years at Braughing, in Hertfordshire. Hundreds of years ago there was a monastery at Braughing and, according to local tradition, five monks from it died one day in May, poisoned by some trout they had fished from a local stream which the abbot had placed out of bounds. "The hand of God" was the verdict in the village—a punishment for poaching; and as if retribution had fallen upon the whole community, the village then fell on hard times. Cattle did not thrive, lambs were eaten by the fox, and crops suffered the blight. This hapless situation lasted for five years.

Then, one night in May, the fifth anniversary of the death of the five monks, their ghosts were seen to walk at Horse Cross; and from that day forward the village prospered.

Every five years afterwards the ghosts of the Braughing Friars seemed to expiate their misdeeds by following this "penance" of a ghostly revisit to the scene of their misdeeds. Right up to the early years of the present century, people of Braughing parish firmly believed that the results of harvests and the village prosperity generally depended on the appearance or otherwise of the ghosts. In the 1920s there were still living older villagers who swore that they had seen the ghosts appear every five years for some fifty years.

But the last time the beneficial phantoms were seen was in 1921. In 1926 they did not reappear, and during the long interval till 1931, manorial lands and farms which formerly were fat and prosperous, failed, and passed into other hands. All the old squires died, and people who were merely wealthy and had no root interest in the locality took their places.

When in 1931 the Braughing Friars still did not reappear it was thought that these changes in the old neighbourhood had had much to do with it; that the penitents' affinity with the district had faded once and for all. Certainly there have been no reports of them being seen since.

THE MUMMY OF MARBURY

Marbury Hall is one of those forlorn old country mansions which one feels at sight must have its ghost—or ought to have. In fact, the haunting attached to this building, tangled in local legend as it is, provides one of the more grotesque of ghost stories.

The ancient manor of Marbury Hall, near Northwich, Cheshire, was largely rebuilt in the 1840s in French style, and was obviously magnificent in its day. Now it has a blighted look, with windows broken, though shuttered from the inside, ornamental stonework missing from the roof, statues lying flat and broken around the garden, and terraced steps overgrown with weeds and grass. A far cry from the time when the mansion's two pointed towers, each topped by a golden ball, rose in elegance over a rich scene.

The house was built on three sides of a large courtyard, with another courtyard at the back approached through a stone archway with a large impressive clock over it. A rose garden flourished on the slope down to the water of Marbury Mere. But the garden now is overgrown, and the Mere, surrounded with reeds, seems attended by sorrowing mists. All that still keep faith with the old house are "Lord Barrymore's pigeons", as the crows, which for countless years have nested at the Hall, are called locally.

Marbury Hall takes its name from the Merbury or Marbury family who formerly owned it, but from the early eighteenth century it became a seat of the Earls of Barrymore, afterwards passing on to the Smith-Barry family, descendants in line, in whose hands it remained until the 1930s.

The ghost of Marbury Hall is a White Lady, whose appearances over many years frightened people living in the locality. Late travellers hurried past the imposing gates of the mansion, never stopping on moonlight nights to look down the long red shale drive to the Hall, for fear of seeing the spectre of a woman on a white horse pass silently by. Right up until recent years there were people returning late at night along lonely Marston Lane or the old Warrington Road who ran home terrified to tell of their encounter with the phantom.

The hauntings by the mysterious White Lady appear to have started some years after the untimely death at the Hall of a lovely, dark-haired French or Egyptian woman. It is said that one of the early Lords Barrymore, an extensive traveller, met the woman during a sojourn in Egypt, and promptly brought her home, rather to the dismay of his family. Whether she remained there as mistress or housekeeper is uncertain. However, when dying, she made a will expressing a wish that her body should be embalmed —a practice then being experimented with by some French and English surgeons—and her body kept at Marbury Hall, of which she had grown very fond. Her wishes were followed, and the mummy was kept in its coffin under the stairboards at the foot of the spiral staircase. The next generation, however, so disliked having it in the house that they had it removed to the family vault at the church of St Mary's and All Saints, at Great Budworth, three miles away.

Soon after this belated "funeral" the hauntings began. Frightened villagers told of seeing the ghost of a lady riding by on a white horse, while at Marbury Hall itself there were many strange incidents, including service bells in the servants' quarters ringing for no apparent reason. The upshot was that the mummy was taken out of the vault and brought back one night through the dark Cheshire lanes to the Hall. The hauntings stopped. Some time later, however, and for the same reason of distaste, the mummy was again taken to the churchyard and "reburied"; but again the hauntings began, and the mummy was brought back to Marbury once more. It was put in a narrow, lead-lined box similar to a monk's chest, which remained in its place under the spiral staircase, near the servants' quarters, until the 1930s.

In 1959, when the *Northwich Guardian* investigated the stories of the White Lady, it found two people at least who remembered seeing the strange coffin. One was Mrs Fanny Weedall, daughter of a maid to the Barrymore family, who as a young child had crept in through the servants' door to see the coffin. Another was Mr Alfred Hayes, in his seventies, who as a young man had seen the bones and wrapping of the mummy.

When, shortly before World War II, the Smith-Barry family vacated the Hall and it was converted into a country club, the head gardener took the coffin and buried it in the rose garden. This might have re-activated the White Lady for a time, for during the war she is said to have been seen by German prisoners at Marbury.

Earlier there had been reports of a "black lady" being seen at Marbury. This is partially explained by the fact that for a long time a housekeeper who always dressed in black lived alone at the Hall and was seen about the grounds at night, which gave rise to some of these stories; yet one man who said he saw the ghost on a number of occasions, and that she definitely was black, was an old villager who worked at the Hall and died not long ago, in his nineties. Whether the Lady did vary her appearances, or whether she became confused with another apparition, cannot be known.

After the war, Marbury Hall was taken over by Imperial Chemical Industries Ltd, who housed some of their workers in the park and Hall. No one reported seeing the ghost from that day forward. The mansion became empty once more in the early 1960s.

Tradition suggests that the horse ridden by the White Lady may be the phantom of Marbury Dunne, the famous mare which belonged to the Smith-Barry family and whose grave is still to be seen in Marbury Park.

Marbury Dunne formed the stake in a wager, and had to run from London to Marbury in the hours between sunrise and sunset. The plucky horse accomplished this, galloping in with time to spare, but during the excitement and confusion, quenched her heavy thirst at a water trough, and the shock killed her. On her grave was placed a stone recording her gallant effort. It bore the words:

> *Here lies Marbury Dunne,*
> *The finest horse that ever run,*
> *Clothed in a linen sheet,*
> *With silver hoofs upon her feet.*

There are, however, some discrepancies in the dates regarding the phantom lady and her supposed steed. The first hauntings appear to have occurred long before Marbury Dunne was alive. So the phantom horse remains as much a mystery as the White Lady of Marbury herself, for there are no records to tell us of the Lady's true identity.

To walk all round the Hall and through the darkest shrubberies on a dark and stormy night, and sit in the abandoned courtyard, causes one to wonder not so much at the ghostly phenomenon as at the vibrant personality of the woman whose wraith it is.

THE ELUSIVE LADIES

There are other elusive ladies. One among them is the Grey Lady said to have haunted Hill Hall, a lonely Elizabethan mansion in Essex, until recent years.

The Grey Lady was active to the end of the 1940s, with a then unbroken history of 350 years of haunting. Very many local people claimed to have seen her sad, gentle figure. She even haunted the nurses' bedrooms when the London Hospital's maternity section was evacuated to Hill Hall during the war. As the mansion's lodge-keeper, Mrs Bingham, said shortly afterwards, "The matron saw her time and again, and if she sees a ghost there is a ghost."

Mrs Bingham's husband was among those villagers who saw the Grey Lady. She said, "Something forced him out of bed one night, and made him walk to a window in a far away part of the mansion to light a cigarette. The ghost walked by. Next morning there was a half-smoked cigarette on the window ledge to show it was not a dream."

The Grey Lady seemed to retreat when plans were made to turn Hill Hall into an open prison. Tradition says that she walked for centuries round bloodstains on the floor of a room in which seven men, all brothers, died in a fight with daggers to win her favours; the brothers were the sons of Sir Thomas Smyth, Secretary of State to Queen Elizabeth, who owned the house in the sixteenth century.

But Sir Thomas had no children except an illegitimate son, who was killed before his own death, while the "bloodstains" have been explained away as damp. Only the continued appearances of the ghost of the Grey Lady have been real enough, though her background remains a complete mystery.

At Winnington, in Cheshire, the last recorded appearance of the ghost of the Winnington Lady was in the 1870s, about a hundred years after her death. In local tradition much is claimed to be known about this beautiful wraith, though there are several versions of the circumstances of her death. The following is considered the most reliable.

In the late 1770s a niece of Lord Penrhyn, the tenant, was preparing to attend a party and ball given in magnificent old Winnington Hall. She was excited, for among the guests being received by her uncle, MP for Liverpool, in the Long Gallery below, was a young man of whom she was very fond.

Her excitement and haste had given her a high colour which was not at all fashionable, and, determined to look her best, she took her lancet to bleed herself a little; it was a method of regaining composure then popular among the ladies. The lancet slipped, and she cut an artery instead of a vein. Frightened by the sight of the spurting blood she dashed out of the room crying for help. She reached the stairs rapidly weakening, and, still moaning for help, collapsed at the foot of the main staircase with helpless guests looking on. She bled to death.

Local people claim that the unfortunate girl afterwards returned to look for her lover, and the tales of Winnington's ghost persist up to the present day. Children are still told of the phantom lady who walks near Winnington Hall, though the last known appearance was so long ago. On this occasion an Irish labourer, finding his way through the new chemical works of Brunner and Mond, was caught up in a mist that swirled into the valley, and suddenly, as he peered into the murky shadows, saw before him a figure of a young woman dressed in white. He turned and fled.

The mysterious lady of Repton Manor, a very old mansion near Ashford, Kent, which was mentioned in the Domesday Book, seemed to continue her hauntings all through the early part of this century and intensify her activities in the late 1940s, when the manor was taken over for a REME Depot, and became the officers' mess.

Shortly after Christmas, 1948 the news leaked out about officers having the lights mysteriously switched on in their rooms at night, and seeing the ghostly figure of a woman bearing a candle pass up the stairs in their quarters. A REME craftsman on guard duty one night also saw the White Lady flitting across a field, and was more frightened by the fact that she appeared to have no feet than by her eerie gliding motion. The guard was turned out to investigate, but the ghost vanished.

Other soldiers and civilians told of seeing strange visions in the gardens.

Local tradition was that centuries ago, a former owner of Repton Manor murdered his wife, and it was her ghost that returned at intervals to haunt the house. On this occasion, however, "Ashford Mary", as the soldiers came to call her, seemed not to be alone, for one officer described the apparition he had seen as dark and cowled, like a monk.

Mr Eric Shepherd, gardener at the manor, was convinced there were two ghosts. He said he had twice seen the ghostly monk in the walled kitchen garden; once at about 5 pm., when it vanished through the wall, and again when, noticing a movement at the end of the garden, he pursued a figure which disappeared into the wall, beyond which there was a 14ft drop. Later, after dark, he and another gardener watched the spot, but saw nothing.

Often in broad daylight, Mr Shepherd said, he and others had been working along the paths and plainly heard approaching footsteps, though nothing whatever was visible.

Sometimes while in the garden he was acutely conscious of a steady, malevolent stare directed on his back, but on looking over his shoulder saw nothing.

Mr H. B. Amos, the previous resident of Repton Manor, said that although he personally had never seen anything uncanny, a friend of his was sure he had seen a ghostly "something" one night as he came up the drive.

Mr Amos's daughter was fully convinced that her old home was haunted. She said that her mother, who had died recently, always assured her that the ghost was harmless, that it liked the occupants and should be accepted as part of the manor and its history. Miss Amos said she had often felt a touch as she went to her room, and had heard rappings, as though of knuckles being struck on the panels of the wall opposite her bed. She had also felt a presence brushing against her.

"Once," she added, "I was sitting at dusk in the same room, with my terrier, when suddenly it gazed at the doorway, its hair stood on end and it leapt in terror through the window. Another time a cat was frightened, apparently by an apparition visible only to itself, but this time in the attic, and it, too, sought escape by the window."

It seemed that Repton Manor might well have two ghosts, one kindly and the other decidedly not.

The phantom lady of Gwrych Castle, near Abergele, North Wales, also walks as the result of a tragedy, according to local belief, and again her true identity is unknown. She is said to be the ghost of a young woman who was thrown from her horse and killed while out riding; she was buried in unconsecrated ground, and is trying to get to consecrated ground. Alternatively, she had been so happy in the castle that she wanted to be buried there, but this was not done as the ground was not consecrated, and so her unhappy ghost has roamed the grounds ever since.

This haunting only dates from the last century, as the castle, with its embattled towers, is not really a very old building. It was built in 1819 in the style of ancient castles, to satisfy a whim of Robert Bamford Hesketh, member of a rich Lancashire family of land proprietors, when he married into the Lloyd family who had squired at Gwrych for generations. The castle, built at great expense, replaced the old Gwrych mansion, a solitary building lying close to the seashore.

Just where the Gwrych Lady fits into the castle's history is obscure, but the more recent accounts of her hauntings date from just after World War II, when the Gwrych Castle estate of some 1,500 acres was sold off in lots by the Earl of Dundonald, into whose hands it had passed.

In 1948 the castle and its furnishings, together with several hundred acres, was bought by Mr Leslie T. Salts, a Liverpool businessman, who went to live there with his wife and two children and converted the building into the popular off-beat holiday and day-trip centre which it is today.

In the spring of 1950 Bruce Woodcock, the British heavyweight boxing champion, chose Gwrych Castle as the training ground for his world title fight with America's Lee Savold. One night in mid-May, Woodcock, while out walking in the ground, with a sparring partner, encountered the Gwrych Lady. This is how his companion, Ted Greenslade, described the incident at the time, fully vouched for by Woodcock:

"Bruce had a bit of supper. Normally he doesn't eat before turning in at ten o'clock, so we decided to take a stroll to walk the meal down a bit. It was about eleven o'clock. We had walked right round the castle when we came to a lonely path and saw the bent-up figure of a young woman sitting on a fallen tree tunk. She had a very pale face and wore a long, dark velvet gown.

"It looked as though she might be in difficulties, so we went up to her. When we got about six yards away she just disappeared. Bruce and I just turned and ran for it; it was the fastest bit of road work we have ever done together."

Mr Salts, after this incident, disclosed that he had been told of the ghost being seen three times in the past eighteen months, always by the old tree trunk.

Others among the several people said to have seen the Gwrych Lady in the early 1950s include Randolph Turpin, who trained there for three months of 1951, and Carroll Levis. Investigators of the Birmingham Society for Psychic Research held a vigil there and, according to their vice-chairman, Mr J. Rowland, in the early morning the watchers saw a luminous form which looked like swirling mist, cross the grass and appear to pass through the castle walls. The phenomenon was accompanied by a sudden rush of cold wind. No natural explanation was found.

Mr Salts tells me that neither he nor any member of his family saw the Gwrych Lady while they lived in the castle, though her various appearances were reported to him in good faith.

Tradition ascribes several other ghosts to Gwrych Castle, which, straggling round the side of a pine-clad hill, looks down on the Irish Sea as well as ancient battlegrounds. These additional spectres are said to be a knight in armour who haunts the battlements and a room in the round tower, a "panting dog", and the ghost of an old Welsh chieftain. They all seem to have their roots in the earlier turbulent history of the locality, where the battles once fought are remembered by such landmarks as one field known as Cae Gerail—"The Field of Corpses". A plaque at the castle states: "On no spot in the Principality has more blood been shed than in this defile."

Another phantom lady who must not be overlooked is one that reputedly haunted a ship, both at sea and in port. The ghost was that of the square-rigged sailing ship, The Lady of Avenel, in the late 1920s the only brigantine left flying the British flag.

The Lady of Avenel, when she lay idle in Leith Harbour during the winter of 1933, had been haunted continuously for seven years. She had a strange history. Built at Falmouth some sixty years before, she had sailed every sea with different cargoes and was at one time used in running slaves from Africa. She had been twice round the Horn, carrying hides, and had sailed on two Arctic expeditions, the last in 1925 with Commander F. A. Worsley, when she was almost crushed in the ice. It was after this trip, for which she was rechristened The Island, that the hauntings began, a female apparition being claimed to haunt her decks. To appease the crew her name was changed again to The Virgo, but this did not stop the ghostly incidents; if anything it intensified them.

On the last voyage of The Virgo the crew spent a very anxious time. A sailor who had never heard of the ghost was reading in his bunk one day when the bunk next to him began to shake violently. There was no apparent explanation. Another time the bosun was reading in his bunk at night when the oil lamp went dim. It seemed probable that the oil reservoir was empty, but on inspection it was found to be full. The wick was turned up again, but time after time the light went dim. Then the bosun kept watch, and was appalled to see a ghostly form "stretch out a long white arm and turn down the lamp".

Another sailor went to sleep with an electric torch under his pillow, and woke with a start when the light from it began to shine in his face. He vowed the torch could not have been switched on accidentally. The same thing happened several times, and he got so scared that he eventually left the ship.

One day at dinner-time the steward heard footsteps on the deck. There should not have been anyone about then, and he went up to check. There was not a soul there. Once at 4 am., said the same steward, he heard a woman's voice on the poop deck, though there was no woman on board.

It was not thought that the haunting would continue when the ship lay idle and up for sale at Leith, but it did. One night the watchman, who was on board alone, could not sleep and sat up reading. Suddenly he saw the ghost of a woman come through a bulkhead and go out again through the cabin door. He would not sleep aboard again, nor would any other nightwatchman stay alone.

The old ship was then bought by Mr F. S. Jackson of Ilkley, a member of the Royal Yorkshire Yacht Club, who took her to Bridlington to be converted into a comfortable cruising yacht. The first thing he did was to give the ship back her old name of The Lady of Avenel.

This seemed to satisfy the mysterious ghost, for the hauntings immediately ceased.

THE MYSTERY OF THE MUSEUM

It was on a Sunday evening in September, 1953 that the drama of York Museum began. A perfectly normal, quiet Sunday. There was a meeting on in the museum and Mr George Jonas, its 44-year-old caretaker, was waiting downstairs with his wife to lock up afterwards. When everyone appeared to have gone, he made a cup of tea before going upstairs to have a last look round and make all secure.

But his wife suddenly asked, *had* everyone gone? Then who was it tramping about upstairs?

Mr Jonas listened, and sure enough heard footsteps. Thinking it must be the curator, he went up to warn him he would be turning out the lights soon. He walked upstairs expecting to see the curator in his office; instead, he found in there an elderly stranger. This is Mr Jonas's account of what followed:

"He was bent over in the far corner of the room. He straightened up as I walked in, turned round, walked past me, and I respectfully drew back. I naturally thought it was some person who had stayed behind. I asked him politely if he was looking for somebody, but he didn't answer. I followed him out of the room, keeping a few steps behind.

"He was dressed, I noticed, in a frock coat with drainpipe trousers, like a professor, and wore elastic-sided boots. I noticed this distinctly as there were no turnups to his trousers. He went straight across into the library, the door of which was open, and I followed him in, turning on the lights as I entered. I heard him exclaim, 'I must find it—I must find it!' He spoke slowly, as if talking to himself.

"He went to a bookshelf and started rummaging among the volumes. By this time I was feeling a bit fed up at being ignored. I thought he must be deaf, so I went up close to him and said, 'If you want to see Mr Willmot (the curator) I'll escort you across to his house.' As I spoke I reached out to touch his shoulder, but when I touched him he vanished . . . just vanished."

It gave the caretaker a terrible shock and he stood transfixed for a minute or two before running to his wife and telling her it was time for them to go. They left for their cottage home in Copman-thorpe, just outside York, not knowing what to make of the extraordinary incident.

Just before the ghost vanished it dropped a book on the floor. Mr Jonas found the volume still lying there the next morning when he looked into the library, and he then told the whole story to the curator.

Four Sundays later Mr Jonas encountered the ghost again. It looked as solid as before—"a very real person"—yet as he watched, the old man in Edwardian dress went through a hall to the library and shuffled *through the locked door*. After this weird episode the caretaker ensured that he had a friend with him on Sundays, so that when, on the next fourth Sunday, the ghost returned yet again, he had a young ex-Guardsman as witness. As they went together into the library, Mr Jonas and his friend heard the pages of a book being turned over, and on walking in they saw a book drop down on to the floor. It was the very same book the ghost had disturbed before.

Mr Jonas was not a nervous man. He had served eleven years in the Army, reaching the rank of sergeant. Before these uncanny incidents he had not believed in ghosts and always classed such things as ridiculous. Now, however, with few people believing his story, he went to his doctor and asked if he could possibly have imagined it all. More than that, he asked the doctor if he would come along to the museum and see for himself. The doctor agreed.

So it happened that on a night of December, 1953 when the ghost was due to appear again—it seemed to be following a regular monthly cycle—a group of six people sat tensely waiting with Mr Jonas in the dimly-lit museum library. They included the doctor and a solicitor friend, also the caretaker's brother, Mr James Jonas —who was among those people strongly sceptical of the haunting —and a representative of the *Yorkshire Evening Press*.

The spacious room with its tall bookshelves had been thoroughly examined beforehand and the blue-backed book which the ghost seemed to make for was inspected by everyone present before be-ing pushed back firmly into place on the shelf. It was an innocuous volume entitled *Antiquities and Curiosities of the Church* and had once belonged to Alderman Edward Wooller, a Darlington solicitor and antiquary, who collapsed and died at a meeting nearly thirty years ago. His business card was pasted inside the book.

The ghostly visitor had always arrived at about 7.40 pm. and shortly before then the watchers took their places. The long minutes ticked by. Then, at exactly eighteen minutes to the hour,

F

the intense silence was broken by a rasping noise as the book was drawn slowly from the tightly packed shelf by an unseen hand and then dropped gently to the floor, coming to rest the right way up and slightly open, close to the rack.

The watchers were overcome with astonishment, all except Mr George Jonas, now greatly relieved at this corroboration of his unnerving experiences. The doctor, who was one of the people nearest to the book, said that a second before it moved his legs had gone strangely cold up to the knees. After the incident he again examined the bookshelf with a torch, removing every book from the shelf, but there was nothing there but a plain wooden shelf and the group were perfectly convinced that there was no natural explanation for what they had just seen. In the words of the doctor, "Without a doubt that book was taken from the shelf by something that is not of this world."

Was the frock-coated ghost of Alderman Wooller walking the museum? Among many letters received by Mr Jonas was one from Miss D. M. Willis, a niece of the alderman living in London. She said that shortly before the apparition made its first appearance she had visited the family grave in a Darlington cemetery; it was her first visit for many years and, she thought, might be responsible for the haunting.

The puzzle of the ghost's identity was, however, the least of it. There was vigorous disagreement within the museum's controlling body, the Yorkshire Philosophical Society, over whether or not the ghostly incidents should be further investigated. The museum's curator for the past four years, Mr F. G. Willmot, maintained an open mind about the various manifestations, now witnessed by a total of nine people, and believed there should be a proper investigation. The Society's chairman did not. He was reported as saying, "It is too silly for words. There will be no investigation. I would not let the subject be brought before the council of the Society. I would not waste time on such tripe."

The clash of opinion led to Mr Willmot handing in notice of his resignation; in the meantime the investigation he had supported went ahead. There could be no January "sitting" because Mr Jonas fell ill, but on the evening of February 7, 1954, the next "fourth Sunday" in the ghostly cycle, twelve investigators waited silently in the museum's shuttered library, its only door locked and elaborate precautions being taken to ensure that no outsiders were near the 100-year-old museum. The watchers included members of the Society for Psychical Research, led by Professor J. W. Harvey of Leeds University, together with two representatives of the Magic Circle, and Mr Jonas himself. They took up their positions at 7.15 pm., twenty-five minutes before the ghost was expected. But although there was a moment when two of the watchers sensed that something was about to happen, both experiencing a sudden feeling of coldness, nothing in fact did; the book which had been disturbed on previous occasions remained wedged in its place. At 8 pm. the ghost-hunters decided to call it a day.

On the next "fourth Sunday", March 7, Professor Harvey led another vigil in the library, with Press and public locked out of the museum grounds as before. Among the six observers who this time sat for forty minutes in the darkened library were the doctor and solicitor present at the original unofficial "sitting", together with Mr Jonas. But again nothing was seen. As one of the observers afterwards said, "Contact with whatever manifestation there might have been in the museum in the past now appears to have been lost."

While all this was going on, strong feeling had been aroused among some members of the Yorkshire Philosophical Society regarding the curator's resignation. It culminated in a special meeting being held to inquire into the circumstances of his going. At this meeting, held the day after the second library vigil, there were, it was reported, "some bitter attacks and some strong defence", and the result was that members, by an overwhelming vote of seventy-seven to twenty-two, decided to ask the curator to withdraw his resignation. Mr Willmot, who had been about to leave for another appointment, agreed to stay, and a crop of resignations came instead from other quarters, the sequel being that at its annual meeting two months later the Yorkshire Philosophical Society emerged with a completely new twelve-member council.

With the ghost retreated and differences over it settled, all was thankfully back to normal at York Museum. The one person, it seemed, to be regretful of this was a grandson of Alderman Wooller in Somerset, who, confirming that the description of the Edwardian ghost tallied exactly with that of his grandfather, expressed himself as being quite thrilled at having a ghost in the family.

THE NIGHT HORSE

The old Royal Ascot Hotel, near the racecourse, once a favourite with the Berkshire race crowds, was put up for auction in the spring of 1964. At the end of the year the demolition men moved in to knock down the old building where the fashionable life had once flourished and guests were met at the railway station by an immaculate coach and pair.

Some of the demolition men made up temporary sleeping quarters in part of the forty-roomed hotel, but work had not long started on the building and its numerous stables, before it became evident to them that something was wrong. There were rumours of "strange goings-on" in the building. Then, shortly after Christmas, the old nightwatchman quit the site hurriedly and vanished without even stopping to collect the two or three days' pay owing to him. He said he had seen and heard a ghostly horse whinnying and stamping late at night in a doorway, and had heard ghostly footsteps.

Other workers then spoke of seeing the phantom white or grey horse, and hearing stamping and snorting in the empty corridors of the derelict hotel; they had also heard the ghostly footsteps. One demolition man, Mr Thomas Murphy, claimed to have seen the ghost horse standing under an arch, while a workmate, Mr Pat Bradshaw, said that sometimes when doing his rounds at night, in the absence of the watchman, he had heard an eerie stamping and snorting in the building which made his hair stand on end. The noises, he said, seemed to start from a small box-room upstairs.

There were other odd occurrences. One night as the men went back to the hotel after finishing work they found themselves unable to open the door; yet it had been left open only minutes before.

The six men then sleeping in the building grew more and more uneasy at night and the site foreman began to find it difficult to get men to work there.

One theory among older residents in the locality was that the ghost grey horse was one of the horses used to drag the bricks up from the kilns to the site when the hotel was built; the unfortunate animal had collapsed from overwork and had to be destroyed. Perhaps, it was thought, after working so hard to help put up the building, it had returned to haunt those who were now pulling it down.

It was a case, however, in which speedy demolition work appeared to bring its own end to the haunting.

A demolition firm of three brothers who contracted to knock down an old country mansion in the Leicestershire village of Bushby, met something more than noises and an apparition, two of them apparently being struck by the ghost or ghosts that lingered on there.

Mr Fred Lunn and his brothers Patrick and Peter, started knocking down the mansion, Bushby Old Hall, in March, 1965. It was a substantial thirty-roomed property built in 1823, and was being demolished to make way for a new housing estate. Its last owner, a tobacco importer with a business in Leicester, had died only months before, and the house was littered with thousands of empty cigar packets.

Trouble began as soon as the demolition work got under way. A strange tapping noise was heard coming from the walls, and ghostly footsteps sounded along a corridor. Then Mr Patrick Lunn, aged thirty-eight, when working in the corridor by himself one evening, was struck by an unseen force. He described the incident:

"I opened six doors in the corridor and walked away from them, and they all slammed shut. There was no breeze or anything that could have caused it. I thought my brothers had crept up on me and were larking about, but I had a look round and could find nobody. I went out on to the roof to look around, and then went back into the corridor, and something hit me between the eyes. I did not see what it was, and it was not so dark that I wouldn't have seen it if there had been anything to see. I did not hang around— I was off like a shot."

He carried the bruise on his face for weeks.

On a later occasion the unseen force attacked Peter Lunn, aged twenty. He said, "I was just getting brass stair clips out of the stairs when I smelt cigar smoke. I knew there was nobody else in the house and I looked up. As I did so, something I could not see hit me in the face and split my lip. I was bowled downstairs by the blow. I got up and searched around, but there was nowhere anybody could have hidden, and there was certainly nobody there."

The brothers made inquiries in the village and learned that the house was reputed to be haunted by the ghost of an old woman who was housekeeper there many years ago, and who had lost her mind and committed suicide by jumping off the roof. A former butler at the mansion told them that the corridor in which Patrick Lunn was struck was in his day haunted by the ghost, which was known as "Mary"; she often walked the corridor and banged the doors shut all at once. But, said the old servant, "Mary" had never harmed anyone before. This gave rise to a belief that there might now be two ghosts active in the building.

There were other incidents. One day as eight of the demolition workers were sitting talking about the mysterious haunting, an upstairs window came hurtling down of its own accord, narrowly missing them. Another time, Patrick Lunn was standing on a low parapet when it suddenly and unaccountably crumbled, sending him crashing to the ground.

One worker stayed only two days at the haunted mansion. He was working in one of the older parts of the building when he suddenly raced down the stairs and out into the garden. He said something about "the old lady" as he went, and that was the last that was seen or heard of him; the frightened man did not return to collect his pay. Two other men after hearing strange noises refused to work on the mansion and had to be drafted to the firm's other sites; another refused to go inside the building. The demolition chief, Mr Fred Lunn, had to search for new workers.

Once again, however, the ghost or ghosts seemed to vanish with the removal of the last brick of the old building, as they did also at Leamington, Warwickshire, in 1960, after demolition men there had narrowly escaped an attack by a seemingly invisible force. The men were knocking down Brookhurst, a hundred-year-old building formerly the clubhouse of Leamington Golf Club, to make way for a block of flats. A gang of four were working on the joists of a top-storey window when suddenly three bricks came crashing through the panes. Glass flew in all directions as the men dived for safety. When they looked to see who or what was responsible for the incident there was no one in sight. It was impossible for children to have thrown the bricks as they were far too heavy for them to handle.

It was, the men said afterwards, a terrifying experience, as if someone was trying to scare them away. One workman refused to go on working alone on the roof. He said he had the strong feeling that there was someone by his side all the time.

The big difference between the Leicestershire and Leamington incidents is that the men at Brookhurst had been warned what to expect when they started the job—that "George" might be busy—but no one had believed the story. They did afterwards, as had many before them who encountered the Brookhurst ghost and reported its strange activities. Dozens of men and women in earlier years had claimed to have heard the ghost. Echoing footsteps which passed through locked doors were heard by groups of people on many different occasions. Doors opened and unlocked themselves, though the keys were always in the safekeeping of one man; lights were switched on and off and the front doorbell rang of its own accord, swift and thorough searches always revealing that mischievous children, burglars or practical jokers could not possibly have been responsible.

Several people claimed that the ghost actually "combed their hair" as they walked down a certain passage. Others who heard something fly past them in the house had each compared the noise with that of a huge bird flapping its wings.

The *Leamington Spa Courier* was able to gather many authentic stories of the ghost from eye-witnesses. Mrs Hilda Heffer, who in the early 1950s was manageress of the golf club and lived on the premises, said that her son, aged twelve at the time, once woke her up in the middle of the night saying he had seen a shadowy object fly across the room, making a great flapping noise as if it had wings, and that it had flown out through the *closed* window. She could not leave the terrified boy alone at night for a long time afterwards.

Mr Granville Gulliman, a Leamington businessman, said he had first become aware of strange things at Brookhurst when he took it over in 1935. He often heard footsteps and sensed that he was being followed, only to find that there was no one there. Sometimes the uncanny presence made a flapping noise which he described as "like a mackintosh blowing in the wind".

Several people recalled when, four times in succession, the front door opened and footsteps passed through the house. No one was found, and though there was deep snow outside there were no footprints.

Mr Gulliman said that on many occasions the police came to lock up for him late at night, only to return first thing in the morning to find the place unlocked. On one occasion in 1948 when a constable called at the club they both heard the sound of someone groaning. They searched the building but could find no one, and the constable was so unnerved that he jumped on his bicycle and pedalled off as fast as he was able.

Mr and Mrs E. T. Gulliman and their young son, who lived at Brookhurst prior to its demolition, said they heard "George" frequently and, although coming in time to accept him as one of the family, tired of answering the doorbell and finding no one there, and of going to meet footsteps which did not have an owner. Mrs Gulliman heard "the wings" at times, while her mother, who also lived on the premises, saw "a winged object" float down the passage.

But the ghost seemed quite harmless, which made its apparent attack on the demolition men so unusual, and perhaps, many thought, a sign of its resentment as being finally deprived of its home.

One of the strangest shocks to any workman in recent years must be that received by Mr Harry Myerthall, a painter's labourer, at Rosyth Dockyard, Fife, in 1955. It happened early one morning when he went to work alone on the aircraft carrier Glory, then undergoing a refit. Mr Myerthall, of Edinburgh, tells his own story:

"A few days after Christmas I left the dining hut near Glory at half-past seven in the morning and went aboard the ship. I went to Cabin 8 on the galley deck where I kept my working clothes. By the time I reached the cabin it was about a quarter to eight. Outside the cabin there was a locker in which I kept my lamp needed for working in the passageways. It was a double lamp that would light both the cabin and the corridor, and I stepped inside the cabin to plug in the cable.

"When the light was switched on I saw a man standing by the dressing-table near the door of the cabin. He was quite tall, about 5 ft 9 in., and was dressed in tropical flying kit. He wore a pair of blue shorts and a leather flying jacket with a fur collar, the jacket hanging open. On the right-hand side of the jacket a row of small bombs was painted in red, and on the left-hand side were pilot's wings. The man had a flying helmet on the back of his head and a wave of blond hair stuck out from under it in the front. On the right side of his neck he had a long red scar. I did not notice if he was wearing flying boots or if the helmet had goggles attached.

"After staring at the man for a moment, I concluded that he was one of the small maintenance staff of naval men aboard the carrier and said, 'Good morning. Did you enjoy your Christmas?' There was no reply to this. I stepped out of the cabin again to get a leather jerkin from the locker, then I suddenly realised it was odd that a man should be in Cabin 8 in full flying kit. I turned round to ask the man who he was, but there was no one in the room.

"I grabbed the lamp which I had hung above the door and rushed into the cabin to search it. There was only a bunk, a dressing-table and an open locker; there was nothing in any of them and no sign of anyone in the room."

He dropped the lamp and rushed along the passage, shouting. As he was plunging down the stairs he was stopped by a workmate who saw his distressed state, and together they returned to the cabin and examined it again, but found nothing and no one.

When the naval commander came aboard, Mr Myerthall and his colleague told the officer about the man with the scarred neck and once again the cabin was searched thoroughly but nothing found.

Mr Myerthall was taken from the ship in a state of shock. Rumour spread through the dockyard that the apparition he had seen was that of an officer who was killed in a crash-landing on the Glory after returning from an operational flight over Korea, shortly before a Christmas during the Korean War. The ghostly airman, it was said, had appeared before, in each case after Christmas and always in Cabin 8, which he was believed to have occupied.

The naval commander, however, said there was no record of a previous manifestation aboard the ship. There had certainly been considerable loss of life among the flying officers of the Glory during her Korean service; in all, twenty-five men had died, but none as a result of a crash-landing on the ship's deck. Nor was it likely that the apparition was that of an RAF officer who was killed, as it was not thought that any RAF personnel had ever served aboard the ship.

So the red scarred ghost of the Glory remains a complete mystery.

THE HAUNTED WARDROBE

On the morning of Thursday, August 19, 1937 the main news of the day was of 300,000 Chinese troops marching to counter a Japanese invasion, Sir Malcolm Campbell all set to capture the world speedboat record, and Tommy Farr besieged while training in America for his heavyweight contest with Joe Louis. What attracted many readers of the *Morning Post*, however, was the following heart-cry tucked away in the Personal Column:

> FOR SALE.—Haunted wardrobe.—Advertiser will be glad to deliver same to anybody interested, complete with ghost, which would also no doubt feel more at home if welcomed.—Write Mrs Barclay, Carterton Manor, Oxon.

Within a few hours of publication more than thirty offers were received by telegram and telephone from many parts of the country. Then the letters started arriving, scores of them.

The strange chain of events which led to Mrs Barclay in desperation placing her advertisement in the national newspaper had begun, innocently enough, three years before, when she looked in at a sale of effects at a private house near Streatley, Berkshire. There she saw the wardrobe in question, a perfectly ordinary piece of Victorian furniture in walnut, seven-foot high and seven-foot six inches wide, with four drawers and mirrors. She paid only £10 for it, for although she was in need of a spacious wardrobe and it took her fancy, there was little of artistic merit in it. She put it in a guest room in her house and thought nothing more of it. There it remained for over two years.

Early in the spring of 1937, Mrs Barclay and the household staff began to hear strange rattling and banging noises in the house, but could not understand where they came from. Then, several friends who at various times came to stay for the weekend asked Mrs Barclay if there was anything odd about the wardrobe. When she expressed her surprise they did not care to explain any more about it; but eventually some guests who slept in the room asked her frankly if she could account for the strange opening and shutting of the wardrobe doors. It had, they said, kept them awake all night.

After her friends' departure, when the weird banging noises continued, Mrs Barclay kept observation and found that the wardrobe doors did seem to be opening and shutting of their own accord. But still she was only half convinced of the wardrobe having any strange properties, and she and her secretary, Mr East, an ex-RAF officer, were inclined to joke about the whole affair. In this mood they decided to investigate the wardrobe for a hidden panel. They went upstairs and walked towards the wardrobe, but before they could touch it, the centre door jumped off of its own accord and smashed the mirror on the door opposite. They were so startled that they decided not to touch the wardrobe at all.

The banging and rattling noises, which could be heard all over the house, now continued almost every night; but that was not all. One night there appeared from the wardrobe the figure of a somewhat bent and wizened man, dressed in old-fashioned clothes and wearing a kind of deerstalker's cap, which walked downstairs and straight out of the front door. Mrs Barclay saw the strange figure when the electric lights were full on. It appeared again on another night, and after the first shock she tried to touch it, but it vanished in her fingers. The ghost continued to make its nightly excursions and she saw it several times. So did her secretary, and her brother. To the three of them together it was its procedure to appear for half a minute or more, then vanish.

Mrs Barclay again tried to touch the ghost, but it slipped from her fingers. On one occasion it stopped and looked at her for a full minute, before turning to the door and walking out, banging the door behind it.

From a chilling phenomenon the ghost now became an out and out nuisance. Mrs Barclay explained at the time, "I am not psychic, nor am I nervous, but this wretched ghost will make such a noise. He clatters across the landing, and shuffles down the stairs, and the noise is often exasperatingly loud."

None of her friends could be induced to spend a weekend at Carterton Manor so long as the wardrobe remained, and her staff threatened to give notice. A friend, Mr E. Rundle, landlord of the Plough Inn at Clanfield, not far away, one night tried lashing the wardrobe up with string, securely fastening it round the doors and drawers. But in the morning the string lay on the floor. The noises continued, the wardrobe drawers opening and shutting all night, and Mrs Barclay had to move her bed out on to the sunshine roof in order to get some sleep.

The ghost seemed to take a dislike to the butler, whom it kicked roundly on the shins. It finally made the life of both butler and maid so unbearable that they gave notice and left hurriedly. It was now clear to Mrs Barclay that she would never be able to get anyone to work for her until the haunted piece of furniture was out of the house. So, just as the cook gave notice that she would not sleep in the house another night, and removed all her belongings to the village, Mrs Barclay decided to put her advertisement in the *Morning Post*, in the hope that someone who could understand ghostly phenomena would take the wardrobe off her hands.

On the day of publication the telephone at Carterton Manor rang incessantly and the rustic calm of the hamlet of Carterton was shattered by the intrusion of eager ghost-hunters, several American visitors calling in their cars to see the ghostly wardrobe. Other offers were for the immediate transport of the wardrobe to country houses hundreds of miles away, while yet others asked Mrs Barclay to name any cash figure she liked.

The ghost apparently did not take very kindly to all this. Mrs Barclay later described how she was just sitting down to lunch, after dealing with the rush of inquiries since breakfast time, when another telegram arrived. It was from Chobham, Surrey, and the sender, in making an offer for the wardrobe, asked, "Can you guarantee ghosts?" Mrs Barclay, by her own account, had a good laugh at this and was about to start her lunch when she heard a noise behind her; and there was the ghost itself, standing in front of the mantelpiece, wearing its deer-stalker cap. It vanished again without a word.

The inquiries and callers came all that day, and there was also the Press to contend with. Mrs Barclay and her secretary agreed to keep a vigil that night with two newspapermen. For an hour nothing happened, then inside the wardrobe there was a noise which one of the witnesses likened to the sound of berries falling off trees. The peculiar noise gradually increased. One of the party, shining his torch, then saw on the floor in front of the wardrobe a button that had not been there before. Suddenly Mrs Barclay screamed, "He is there!" None of the others then glimpsed the ghost, but Mrs Barclay said she had seen it quickly leave the room, wearing as usual its deer-stalker hat.

Not long afterwards there was a loud cry from outside the house and a six-foot figure in white could be seen bobbing about in the vicinity; the practical jokers were now at work. The intruder was chased off the grounds by Mr East.

Mrs Barclay and her secretary then decided to have the wardrobe moved out into the garden, so that all could get some rest.

Next day the stream of letters and telegrams continued to pour in from places throughout the country; making offers, giving advice, and including even a proposal of marriage. Telegram after telegram asked for the wardrobe to be reserved. A college of astrology wanted it; so did four spinsters, who asked to be allowed to have the ghost to protect them as they lived alone in a large house; while another letter asked, "Do you think the ghost would be happy in a small modern house?"

Then there was the flood of advice. "I should say it's doubtful if the ghost will go with the wardrobe. He shows himself to you as you are sympathetic, but he may not do so to others. . . . Don't lock the wardrobe, you should never lock a door on a corpse or a ghost. . . . Leave the door open at night so that he can come in and out, and put a nice comfortable chair beside it for him, as he clings so to the wardrobe. . . . I should say his treasure is concealed somewhere inside it. I should search until you find out what it is. . . . Never mind the cook, cooks are plentiful, but you can never get another wardrobe like this."

Mrs Barclay's one fear was that the ghost would not agree to its enforced removal and depart with the wardrobe, but would stay on in the house, in which case she herself would have to leave. Resolute to have the wardrobe off the premises at the earliest moment, she accepted an offer of £50 from her friend Mr Rundle at Clanfield—it was the highest of a number of early bids she received—and the wardrobe was transported the few miles south to its new home at once.

Mr Rundle put the wardrobe in an outhouse in the garden of his inn. The Plough was then being rebuilt and there was as yet no room large enough for the wardrobe. But, said Mr Rundle, an ex-RAF officer, he would have his own bedroom enlarged and put the wardrobe in it, then anyone who would like to sleep in the room would be free to do so. He emphasised, however, that he personally had no belief in ghosts.

Nor, unfortunately, had the more boisterous elements in the neighbourhood, for no sooner did peace come to Carterton, with an end to the jokers in white sheets running about firing pistols near the manor, than pandemonium reigned in the village of Clanfield. News of the wardrobe's arrival soon spread and all the lads from miles around gathered round the outhouse and began catcalling and throwing bricks on to the iron roof. It was impossible for a long time for the residents of the Plough even to hear themselves. One or two of the village youths in all seriousness asked to be allowed to sit round the wardrobe and keep watch, and they were given peace for a few minutes, but then the majority outside restarted catcalling, wailing and throwing brick-bats, and the "sitting" was a failure.

Mr Rundle, though still stressing his scepticism, testified that during one of the quiet spells on this first night one of the ward-robe's doors started trembling considerably; and there was no question of vibration coming from anywhere as the outhouse walls were of two-feet thick Cotswold stone. His wife, too, heard curious rattlings and a "noise like an aeroplane" coming from the wardrobe.

On the next night the row from the villagers was worse than ever, so in the morning Mr Rundle had the wardrobe brought into the hotel and put into the one available room. As it had been strongly suggested that the ghost was seeking something in the wardrobe, he took it to pieces. He found nothing abnormal—and certainly no bloodstains, as had also been claimed. A furniture expert also examined the wardrobe, finding nothing except some signs of alteration inside.

From that day on the wardrobe remained silent. Mr Rundle was left with an ordinary utilitarian piece of Victorian furniture; and wherever the unknown figure in the deer-stalker hat might have departed to, it never again visited Carterton Manor or bothered anyone at the Plough.

THE SAD CAVALIER

Soon after taking over the Ring o' Bells, a very old public-house in Middleton, near Oldham, in December 1966, Mrs May Penneyston began to hear footsteps in the passage, though when she went to look there was never anyone there. Frequently on hearing the footsteps she would think it was a customer, but on going into the bar would find it empty.

There were other puzzling incidents. Mrs Penneyston was often woken up in the night by bumping sounds, as if someone was trying to get in, but when the premises were searched everything was found to be in perfect order. One night she was woken by a big crash like the sound of windows breaking, but again, on a search downstairs, there was no one there and nothing to account for the noises. On yet another night she heard strange rustling sounds, which she thought at first might be her son moving about, but it was not, and once again there was nothing to explain the disturbance.

Meanwhile the mysterious footsteps continued their wandering at all times of the day and night; as they still do.

Mrs Penneyston is now firmly convinced, as others before her have been, that the centuries-old public-house is haunted by the ghost of the "Sad Cavalier", a local Royalist who is believed to have been murdered and buried in the cellar there in the days of Cromwell.

The Ring o' Bells goes much farther back into history than the time of the Civil Wars. Its foundations, like those of the church nearby, are believed to date from Saxon times, and a Druid's temple is thought to have once stood on the site. Later, and until the dissolution by Henry VIII, the Bells served as the refectory to the church and monks brewed their beer there. In Cromwell's day there still existed a secret passage from the cellar to the church, and it was this passage that played a prominent part in the fate of the Sad Cavalier.

The cavalier, tradition says, was the son of Lord Stannycliffe of Stannycliffe Hall, near Middleton. Father and son were staunchly

Royalist, whereas Middleton was a powerful stronghold of the Roundheads. Cromwell's men used as their headquarters the Old Boar's Head, which still stands not far away on the main road to Rochdale. The Royalists were obliged to meet secretly in the Ring o' Bells cellar, which then formed the public-house itself.

One day while the cavalier was in the cellar someone betrayed him to the Roundheads. He escaped hurriedly through the secret passage to the church, but the Roundheads, who, some say, made their own way to the church through another passage from the Old Boar's Head, intercepted him at the church and cut him down. It seems uncertain whether the cavalier was actually killed inside the church or whether, left for dead, he managed to drag himself back through the passage to the Ring o' Bells' cellar, where he died; but at any rate tradition is firm that he was buried by his friends under a flagstone in the cellar.

Today, in a little "snug" above the cellar where the cavalier is supposed to lie buried is what is known as the Cavalier's seat. Mrs Penneyston tells me, "Some people who had not heard about the ghost have complained about feeling cold and having the shivers when they sit there, though it is warm everywhere else and there is no draught." Other customers, she adds, have refused to sit there at all, including one man who said he would not do so for £100. The ghosts of the Royalists are supposed to sit around the table at this spot at night; it is referred to as "the ghosts' table".

Other occupants of the Ring o' Bells have, over the years, reported seeing the cavalier, dressed in a wide-brimmed plumed hat, lace collar and cloak, and carrying a sword. Mrs Penneyston has not seen the apparition but she has a strong feeling that the ghost is there always. She describes him as "friendly but terribly sad", and says she thinks he likes to mix with the customers. There have been many instances of this. Once, when a customer went to the bar for a drink, he made way for someone apparently trying to pass him, yet on looking round found there was no one there. Another time a customer heard someone laughing at the back of Mrs Penneyston, a hearty "Ha, ha, ha," but again there was nobody there.

Mrs Penneyston's husband, Duncan, keeps an open mind about the ghost but he admits to once hearing a voice in the cellar that he could not explain. He was in the cellar when he heard footsteps coming downstairs and a voice, very deep, saying "'Ow do you do?" apparently behind him. Mr Penneyston replied "I'll be with you in a minute", and continued for a moment looking for something in an old cupboard. When he looked round there was no one there, nor was there anybody in the public-house at all.

This occurred on one of the nights that Mrs Penneyston heard the ghostly footsteps in the passage.

Mrs Penneyston considered having the cellar flagstone lifted and the floor dug up in a search for the cavalier's grave. She thought that on the one hand it would show if there was any truth in the legend, which seemed well supported by the discovery in recent years of at least one secret tunnel and helmets, pikes, and other weapons; while on the other hand it might give rest to the cavalier if, should his bones be found, they were given a proper burial in the churchyard.

But on second thoughts she decided against having the cellar floor disturbed. The cavalier, she now believes, might prefer to remain in peace in the place where he was buried. She looks upon him as a friendly sort of ghost and says he does not frighten her at all.

"The tune of 'Greensleeves' is supposed to have been the sort of theme of the cavaliers," she told me. "Apparently they used to whistle the tune to identify themselves. One day I was sitting at the piano and found myself playing it. It just happened. I often play it now; I think he likes it."

The only person now in the locality who is said to have actually seen the cavalier's ghost is Mrs E. Peacock, who lives in an old cottage nearby. She had to be up very early one morning to deliver papers and suddenly came upon a man in a slouch hat and dress of the cavalier period. His dark brown hair was in ringlets and he had a very sad face and was crying, she says. He came towards her, and then vanished just as suddenly as he had appeared.

Another case of encountering a ghost almost immediately on moving into the premises occurred at Kidderminster in 1963, although here there was no local tradition to explain the sudden haunting.

Within weeks of taking over as bar manager at the licensed premises in Swan Street of Charles Harvey and Co, more popularly known as Harvey's wine vaults, Mr Bert Pye began to hear footsteps when there was no one but himself in the building. Then there were several other uncanny incidents, including mysterious bangings and doors opening and shutting of their own accord, which prompted Mr Pye to stay no longer than necessary after closing the bar each night.

On one alarming occasion a customer was sitting alone in a room at the back of the premises when one of the doors suddenly opened and closed; then the latch on another door which led out

G

to the street was raised and the door opened by itself *against a spring*. It just seemed, Mr Pye told me, as if someone had walked across the room from the one door to the other. The startled customer left his drink and the premises rather hurriedly.

Shortly afterwards one of the barmaids, Mrs Winifred Mac-Donough, saw the ghost. One afternoon after closing time she was clearing up on one side of the bar when she heard footsteps. Thinking someone had been accidentally locked in, she went to check around. There was nobody there, but as she turned to go back she was surprised to see the figure of a woman suddenly coming towards her round the bar.

Mrs MacDonough described the woman as being tall, young, and smartly dressed. "She was wearing a long brown dress with ruffled collar, pulled in tightly at the waist, and a straw hat. I still thought she was a customer and then I realised she was wearing clothes from another century. She had a friendly face and I wasn't frightened. She seemed to float past and then disappeared through the side door."

A second barmaid also experienced a visit from the mysterious Lady in Brown. The big puzzle was, who *was* the restless phantom?

It seemed that the cellar at Harvey's, which was used for wine and spirit storage, might provide a clue. The *Kidderminster Times* recalled the surprise discovery of this cellar in 1851. The Harvey's building was rebuilt on the site of the former Clarence Inn, and in 1851, when this inn's stable flooring was being repaired, it gave way to disclose a great vault below containing a two-foot deep layer of decayed animal matter and human bones. It seemed that the vault had been filled with the human remains and then arched over, for the bricks of the arch were of much later date. Finds among the rubbish included a small black bottle, an old drinking glass, a clumsy pick-axe and some heavy tobacco pipes of an unusual shape.

Historians believed that the vault, which had a pointed roof and gothic windows with mullions of the sixteenth century, was at one time a chapel belonging to an old gild, or perhaps the chapel to a private manor house nearby. Whether there was any connection between the chapel and the Lady in Brown it was impossible to say, but the report of the haunting brought word from Mr Arthur James, who years ago had lived over a shop adjoining Harvey's premises. Mr James said his family then had use of the vault, which had been adapted as cellars, and often the atmosphere in there felt rather strange; his sister was afraid even to go past the entrance. But although he lived there for about six years, Mr James never heard or saw anything of the ghost.

Unlike the Lady in Brown, whose appearance seemed short-lived, a crinolined ghost that walked the old Volunteer Inn at Frenchgate, Doncaster, in the 1950s was very consistent in her haunting. Nor was she entirely unknown, local belief being that she was the spirit of a young woman who had died in the inn after a fall from her horse in the courtyard 200 years ago.

The licensee, Mr George Greetham, and his wife did not believe in ghosts when they first moved into the inn; until they saw what they described as a "crinolined shadow" moving about the corridors and bedrooms. Mr Greetham said the ghost's features were so delicate that he and his wife were not a bit scared, and in time, like Mrs Penneyston with the Sad Cavalier, they grew rather attached to the wraith; so much so that when the Volunteer Inn was due for demolition to make way for a road scheme, they became anxious to find her another "home", and seriously considered whether the ghost, whom they called "Cynthia", could be transferred somewhere else by clairvoyance; preferably to a public-house, as the ghost seemed to like mixing with the customers.

Mrs Greetham described her as "such a sweet ghost. She wanders about and never bothers anyone."

Many ghosts can be just like that.

THE PHOTOGRAPHIC GHOST

In the little mid-Devon village of Spreyton, on a pleasant sunny day in 1932, the vicar, together with a friend, walked out on to the vicarage lawn, the vicar carrying his inexpensive box camera. In turn each took a snapshot towards the vicarage; and the resultant pictures began arguments that went on for years afterwards.

In each case there appeared in the photograph the shadow of what seemed to be a monk, kneeling some five or six feet from the photographer, apparently in prayer, and wearing a flowing robe and cowl.

At the time of day the pictures were taken, and from the standing position of each photographer, it would have been impossible for the sun to cast a shadow in front of them. Yet the "manifestation" was quite clear in both pictures, the cowled head being perfectly distinct. In the picture taken by his friend, the vicar, the Rev W. R. Dunstan, was seen standing in front of the house. Any possibility of the monk being Mr Dunstan's shadow was disposed of by the fact that Mr Dunstan was wearing jacket and trousers, while the mysterious shadow was undoubtedly that of someone in a long robe. In addition the vicar was a small man, while the strange figure whose shadow appeared in both photographs was of unusually large build.

The pictures were carefully examined by experts, who could offer no explanation for the ghostly monk. The developers, too, could detect nothing abnormal about the film or the camera, which were both perfectly ordinary.

It was an eerie shock for the vicar and his friend, but stranger things were witnessed inside Spreyton vicarage, a building centuries old. Mr Dunstan described them:

"One evening I called in my sexton on some business or other, which we were attending to in an upstairs room. Suddenly, heavy footsteps crossed the hall, directly below us. They were calm, unhurried and deliberate, and we sat amazed, for we knew there could be no other human being in the house. The moment they ceased we leapt up and ran downstairs, but there was no one there. The poor sexton was very puzzled. He had heard rumour of such things in the village but had been sceptical about their veracity; now he is prepared to swear that he heard the footsteps.

"On another occasion my wife and I had retired for the night and I had gone soundly to sleep, when the phantom footsteps manifested themselves. My wife tells me that she plainly heard the footsteps cross the hall, mount the stairs, pass the bedroom door, and enter the next room, where some clothes were drying on a clothes horse. At this point there was a report, exactly as if the clothes horse had gone over. The noise awakened me, and after my wife told me what she had heard, we both went into the next room to see what was there. But as usual, there was nothing—and the clothes were just where they had been.

"These things never startle us, however; on the contrary, we are quite used to them, and at each incident wonder interestedly what the next will be. Often we will hear a chair or something fall in another room. We will know by the sound exactly what has fallen over, and yet never, on inspection, have we found anything out of its place.

"Once I was sitting reading when I heard the letter-box bang, as it always does with the post, and I heard something fall flat on the floor. I went straight to the hall, a couple of steps, but there was nothing there—absolutely nothing."

Though the ghostly footsteps and other strange noises continued at the vicarage for some time, no apparition was seen apart from that apparently captured by the box camera. Nor was there a conclusive explanation for the haunting, despite lingering memories in the village of similar disturbances at the vicarage reported by a vicar many years before. Mr Dunstan's two immediate predecessors had heard nothing beyond the scurry of rats, the flutter of nesting bats in the roof timbers, and the activity of bees settled in the corridor walls. The only slender clue to the haunting provided by history was that in 1445 the priest of the parish was Henry Le Mayne, a Norman, whose name was supposed to be a corruption of *le moine*, which meant "the monk".

Spreyton vicarage, however, was not alone with its ghost. Close by stood rambling Bush House, the biggest house in the village, with no fewer than four staircases leading to its upper rooms. Attached to this building, which was at least 400 years old, was a legend that if one followed the ghost of a woman in a black silk dress, she would lead the way to a vast sum of money stowed away in one of the nooks and crannies that abounded in the place. No one as yet had had the courage to test the truth of the legend, though the Black Lady was by no means as elusive as the spirit of the vicarage and appeared fleetingly at intervals. She had last been seen only two years before, in 1930, by two girls staying in the house, and her practice seemed to be first to attract attention by the loud rustling of her dress, and then to emerge from an old cupboard in a corner of a room in which stood an old style four-poster bed.

There was, however, nothing to suggest that the Black Lady had transferred her attention to the vicarage, and certainly her apparition bore not the slightest resemblance to the monkish figure in the vicar's photographs.

About this same time another vicar told of how he had wit-nessed the activities of a spectral nun. This was at the old village of Monkton, in Pembrokeshire. The vicar, the Rev Tudor Evans, and his family had to live for a time in the Old Hall, which was believed to be part of an ancient priory; some of the rooms had been cells, and there was a large groined crypt under it. Mr Evans said that for some time he heard a heavy knocking on his bedroom door regularly at four o'clock every morning and it could not be traced to any normal cause. There was one room into which the family's dog refused to go; one day his daughter saw a glow in this room and the distinctly outlined head and shoulders of what looked like a cowled figure, leaning out of the window and apparently waving to her. On another occasion, said the vicar, a friend who slept the night in the haunted room heard the rustling of garments round his bed all night, and when he tried to light candles they were mysteriously snuffed out.

Evidence in support of this haunting was the discovery of the kneeling body of a woman walled up in the priest's room of Monkton Church. The vicar believed she was a nun who had committed some sin that had kept her spirit earthbound. It had been, perhaps, her task to wake the other nuns for a four o'clock service, and this her wraith was still continuing to do.

The ghost of a nun seen in the 600-year-old rectory at South-fleet, near Gravesend, was also believed by the rector, the Rev William Falloon, to be that of a woman who had sinned. This ghost had actually been exorcised by the Bishop of Rochester many years before, in 1874, but apparently with little success, for during his twenty-one years at Southfleet until retirement in 1953, Mr Falloon several times saw the nun in her brown habit walk from the monk's room of the rambling old rectory. Mr. Falloon, who described the nun as having the red face of a country-woman, thought it possible that she had associated with a monk whose gravestone had been uncovered near the church nearly a century before; the monk had been excommunicated, obviously for some terrible sin.

In the fine old Queen Anne rectory at Ash, near Aldershot, a shock for the rector, one night of 1938, was not the sight or sound of a wandering figure but the noisy appearance of a phantom vehicle which passed right through his bedroom. The Rev W. J. Blaikie told in his parish magazine how he was suddenly woken from his sleep by the noise of a post horn and galloping horses; next thing, wide awake, he saw a stage coach and four rush up and clatter through his bedroom in the direction of St Peter's Church.

"No one," he said, "was more surprised than I at being awakened by the noise of a horn and the thud of horses and seeing this strange apparition canter through the house. I both saw it and heard it quite distinctly—it was most realistic."

Ash Rectory, with its old cobbled coaching yard attached, was built on the site of an old coaching road and, Mr Blaikie thought, the coach-and-four, apparently resenting this intrusion on its right of way continued to drive through the rectory as if it did not exist. On making inquiries Mr Blaikie discovered that the previous rector had witnessed the very same noisy passage of the spectral coach.

As might be expected, vicarages have many times been thought to be haunted by their late incumbents. A recent case was at Deddington, Oxfordshire, in 1962 when mysterious happenings at the vicarage were attributed to the restless spirit of the late vicar, the Rev Maurice Frost, who had died on the Christmas Day previously, aged seventy-three. Mr Frost, who had been vicar of Deddington for thirty-five years, was a collector of antique clocks and kept about a dozen of them at the vicarage, always making sure that they all chimed together. When Mr H. Campbell-Jarratt moved into the vicarage nearly four months after the vicar's death, to settle his cousin's affairs, he decided to sell the clocks. They then all began striking at 4 am., though they had not been wound since the vicar's death.

The chimings stopped when the clocks were taken away to be sold in London. But there were other odd happenings. Strange noises were heard in the ground floor rooms of the vicarage, especially in the study, usually between 3.30 am. and 9.30 am. Mr Campbell-Jarratt never saw the ghost but, he said, for a long period the feeling was always there that someone was in the place all the time. Once when he was leaving a room carrying an antique handle, the handle was suddenly wrenched back in his hand. He tried to walk on but was pulled backwards; he was forced to drop the handle and walk away. On other occasions beds were pressed down as if someone was sitting on them beside his wife and himself; he heard footsteps in the vicar's study when no one was there; domestic staff heard coughing in the empty study, and gave notice. This coughing was also heard in the drawing-room, and the late vicar had been a chain smoker. Then there were instances of pictures being disturbed; once, while a visitor was being shown round the vicarage, a picture which was in its proper position was later seen to have been turned round.

The incidents stopped shortly before the auction sale at the vicarage, but so often in these cases a service becomes necessary.

In 1931 a Roman Catholic priest in Eccles, Lancashire, decided to offer prayers and sprinkle holy water in a house claimed to have been haunted for four years by one of his predecessors. The Lees family had spent two uneventful years in the house in Liverpool Road, Eccles, before the ghostly incidents began. First Mrs Lees herself became aware of them, then other members of the family, and friends. There were strange noises in the night, and members of the family wakened in the early hours to find their beds moved from the positions in which they had been when they went to sleep. Then there came, at intervals, a figure in priest's clothing which was seen to move down the stairs and disappear through a wall. The ghost's appearance was usually followed by more odd noises.

The family eventually had to move out of the rooms in which the phenomena was most pronounced, though the apparition continued to visit all rooms of the house at night, dissolving into nothing when challenged. Two girls sprinkled holy water in an attempt to lay the ghost, but the disturbances continued and frightened visitors to the house, one at least of whom clearly saw the ghost walk through the wall at the bottom of the stairs.

Neighbours were convinced that the apparition was that of Father Sharrock, the first Catholic parish priest of Eccles, who had died at the house, then the presbytery, forty years previously. This fact of the ghost's probable identity made the Lees family all the more reluctant to take action and it was a friend who finally approached Father J. Drescher, the parish priest of St Mary's, and told him the whole story. Father Drescher decided the Lees needed help. So, on an October afternoon of 1931, he went into each room of the house, sprinkling holy water and murmuring blessings to allay the fears of the occupants; and prayers for the family and the dead priest were also said in the old church.

This seemed to give the ghost of Father Sharrock release at last.

THE HOUSE OF SPOOK WATER

Mr Samuel Long and his wife had lived quietly for thirteen years in their house in Bell Lane, Leicester. It was a comfortable enough house and certainly had no signs of damp; in fact it was commonly acknowledged to be the driest of all of the properties in the road.

There had been just one spot of bother for the Longs, in the twelfth year of their tenancy. This was when a new floor was laid in the kitchen and soon afterwards began to flood with water. At first the sink outlet was thought to be at fault, but it was found to be quite sound. A plumber eventually cured the flooding by putting an air brick under the floor; he said he believed there was a hidden spring below the house.

There was no more trouble and the incident was soon forgotten. Some eighteen months later, however, in the long hot summer of 1933, the peace of the neat house in Bell Lane was disturbed in the most distressing manner.

Mr Long was a retired hotel barman of seventy-four, in such perfect health and vigour that he looked at least ten years younger; his wife Annie, an active woman in middle-age, went out daily to work, and they had an adopted daughter aged thirteen. They also let one of the rooms to a lodger.

One August day, during one of the worst droughts in Leicester for years, Mr Long was startled to find water coming unaccountably from a bedroom ceiling. He thought it must be due to a leak in the roof, though with no heavy rain having fallen in weeks it was very puzzling. The water stopped as mysteriously as it began, but then came another inrush in the front bedroom, which saturated the bedclothes and flooded the floor to such an extent that he had to double up the linoleum like a trough and run off the collected water from it into a tin bath. Again the water abruptly stopped, and the ceiling where it had come through was immediately dry and perfectly unmarked.

Then came an outbreak in the back bedroom, over the landing. Hearing a hissing noise, Mr Long rushed in and found his young daughter playfully enjoying a light shower bath in a spray of water which was issuing from the wall. Water then began pouring from the bedroom ceiling, in such volume that it overflowed from the floor and cascaded down the stairs; it also spouted from the wall over the fireplace in the living room downstairs, as well as from the wall opposite; and always it stopped as suddenly as it began and the points on the ceilings and walls from which it had poured were quickly dry and the wallpaper absolutely unmarked.

Everything the water fell on, however, did not dry instantly in the same remarkable fashion. As Mr Long went on to collect more than ninety bucketsful of water from the various outpourings all manner of the family's belongings, including the piano, were damaged; kindly neighbours stored some of their furniture and the rest they tried to protect with brown paper, but with all of the bedding in the house saturated Mr Long's wife and daughter had to go to neighbours' houses to sleep, while he and the lodger stayed up for three nights to deal with any fresh outbreaks. There were none, but then Mr Long and the lodger also left the house while the corporation's experts examined it.

Earlier, the reaction of one water inspector to Mr Long's urgent call had been that the flooding must be due to a burst pipe to the bathroom, or a leaking tank. But when he got to the house he found it had no bathroom and no tank, neither was there any trace of water pipes in the wall of the roof space. Water erupted from a wall as he made his survey, but still he could not trace the source of it. Another water inspector then came to question the family and examine the premises, and he was nearly knocked down by a sudden stream of water when he tried to mount the stairs.

The mystified water men now sought the help of the city's health and building departments, and while the family lodged with neighbours a group of experts searched the house. The most curious aspect of it all was that some of the water had been claimed by the Longs to have come from a wall only 4½ inches thick, a single brick wall. Mr Long scorned all the suggestions of ghosts or other psychic phenomena which were put forward and maintained his belief that a hidden spring, as mentioned by the plumber, was the possible cause—it was, he thought, forcing its way up the walls to find an outlet. But against this a city water engineer said that if such was the case, why was not water forced out into rooms of the adjoining houses?

The corporation officials did a thorough job. Bricks were loosened from the walls and found to be quite dry and the walls perfectly sound. Skirting boards were removed and floors tested. But there were no signs of water anywhere, not even in the cellar, though here it was seen that the pressure of water from the flooded floors above had broken down plaster from the cellar ceiling.

A city engineer now blamed the house sparrows. He suggested that the spouting of the house had possibly been blocked up by the nests of sparrows, and that half an inch of rain which had fallen in two days recently had accumulated in the roof space. It had probably overflowed down the walls and, finding the weakest places, spurted out into the rooms.

The truth was, however, that no one really knew how the water had got into the walls and mysteriously poured out of them, gallon after gallon of it, in the middle of a serious drought.

So the Longs returned to their home. Not once in their absence had the "spook water" been seen to flow, but now, immediately they moved in, it began again. A reporter of the *Leicester Evening Mail*, as he entered the house, was astonished to see water streaming down the walls of the living room. The piano was saturated, and the water had penetrated into cupboards.

"The floor was flooded, and Mr and Mrs Long were unable to sit down to a meal because of the water which streamed down upon them. I was taken upstairs and only just dodged a shower of water which fell from the ceiling of the landing. All the beds have had to be covered with waterproofs, which hold pools of water. Amid the scene of desolation, Mrs Long's young daughter tried vainly to eat her meal in comfort, but was continually disturbed by water falling on her food and drenching the table. Mr Long said that the water generally stopped flowing about nine o'clock in the evening, and the walls were soon perfectly dry, without any signs of disturbance."

Among other visitors to the house that day were detectives of the Leicester City Police. Mr Long had kept a diary of the outbreaks, which on some days had occurred nearly every half hour, and they examined this and made a thorough search of the house but, like the building experts, failed to suggest a solution. The jets of water began to play again after the police had left, as they did after a further visit by the architect, who re-examined the property without result.

Some people now firmly believed that the unfortunate family—or one among them at least—were attracting uncommon psychic phenomena, though the more general opinion was that there must be a rational explanation, if the only way of deciding it was to demolish the house.

The Longs continued to live a hand-to-mouth existence trying to dodge the frequent spouting. Two days after the visit from the police the water was more active than ever, seemingly following

Mr Long about the house all day. As soon as he went into a room, water would pour from the ceiling and out of the walls, all over the floor. Several times he was drenched, while every article of furniture was thoroughly soaked. In desperation he went out into the garden and sat on a stool near the house, but in seconds he was soaked again as water shot from the *outside* wall down his neck. When he jumped up and stepped back the water spouted again all over him.

Unable to endure it any longer Mr Long and his wife made arrangements to move out and stay temporarily at the house next door, occupied by Mr and Mrs J. Worrald and Miss Evelyn Law; and the following day they shifted their belongings in. But in less than an hour the Worrald home was also visited by the water. An *Evening Mail* photographer happened to be in the house at the time and to his amazement saw a jet of water issue through the wallpaper, pour over a picture and splash on to the fire. At the same time Miss Law ran downstairs shouting that water was pouring into the upstairs rooms. The water, reported the photographer, soaked through the roof, poured down the wall and on to the floor "like a cascade coming out of nowhere".

Miss Law was in a bedroom when the water first spurted out at her. She said, "I jumped away but the bed was covered. The walls were quite dry a minute after. I went on to the landing and the water had come through the ceiling there. It ran down the walls and left them dry, but gathered in a pool on the floor".

All this happened just after Mr Long had finished putting his furniture into a room—the water spouted from the walls the precise moment he took a seat in his neighbours' kitchen. Happily, no more water came after this surprise upset, and, next door in the Longs' house, there was only one more outbreak, which occurred when Mr Long visited it to get some belongings. After that all was quiet. The brewery which owned the house now took a hand and sent officials to lock it up so that the premises could be thoroughly searched and inspected again. The doors and windows of the deserted building were carefully sealed pending the investigation.

It had now been suggested that someone was throwing buckets of water over the walls, but, said Mr Long, that was ridiculous. Nobody bore them any malice and certainly no member of his family wished to break up the home. Besides, all the many other witnesses of the phenomenon could not have been fooled. It now seemed possible that there was a spirit loose in the house but he did not know what to think; the one thing certain was that he and his family had been driven out of their home.

For some three weeks the troubled house in Bell Lane was kept under observation by experts called in by the brewery. An inspection was carried out each day, but there was no sight or sign of the "spook water". Mr and Mrs Long were told that the phenomenon had definitely ceased, and so on an October day they moved their belongings in again.

All was peaceful in the kitchen after the furniture had been carried in, and Mr Long was making some tea, when suddenly a powerful jet of water shot from the ceiling, drenching the floor, the table, the tea things, and the opposite wall. This was the start of yet another onslaught. Mr Long was soaked by water which frequently shot across the room from the ceiling—the force of it broke four gas mantles; three times his wife came home from work to find the kitchen so full of water that she could not have her dinner. Again there were several other witnesses to the inexplicable outbreaks. One was a workman who was taking the top off a wardrobe in a bedroom when water suddenly spurted from the wall and hit him in the face; another was a newspaper reporter seeking the latest developments, who arrived to find Mr and Mrs Long standing gloomily in the kitchen with the floor drenched with water, and the table and a mirror on the wall heavily splashed; while still on the ceiling was the wet patch, rapidly drying, from which the water had poured not long before he entered the house. Walls, floors and ceilings were always very quickly dry and at the start of every day the house was bone dry from top to bottom.

It seemed clear that the family could not go on living in the house and Mrs Long insisted that they should move, though it was difficult to find comparable rented accommodation in such a hurry. As Mr Long made efforts to do so, however, the water mysteriously stopped and the family experienced an uneasy peace. The lull lasted just eleven days. Then, one Sunday, Mrs Long was sitting in her living room when water suddenly began to pour from the ceiling, thoroughly soaking her. It flooded the living room and the kitchen and then spouted in further jets from the ceiling and walls, and she had to cook the dinner wearing her mackintosh and rainhat.

Police called at the house again and searched every inch of it, but left no wiser than before. It was now nearly mid-November and the distressed family had been battling against the "spook water" since August.

Mr Long said plaintively, "People are saying that we have done it ourselves because we want to get a council house, but that is not true. Why should we wilfully ruin our home? We had just had part of the house redecorated and we should not have done that if we had wanted to leave. I have tried everywhere to get another house, but I cannot find one. I wish someone could get one for us. This thing is driving us mad."

It was at this point, with the family prepared almost to walk the streets rather than endure the constant showers, that the outbreaks of the "spook water" began to lessen. Days passed without a single flooding, and when the water did come, at intervals, the jets seemed very much weaker. Finally, during the winter months the showers stopped completely, as mysteriously as they had begun. The house became perfectly dry again, and remained so up to Mr Long's death in 1936, and after.

THE GHOST BUS OF KENSINGTON

It was in the summer of 1933 that talk of a mysterious "ghost bus" seen hurtling by in the early hours first began to spread among the residents of North Kensington, London. People who had, until then, kept secret their own glimpse of the strange vehicle, for fear of ridicule and their own sanity, were relieved to find, as the matter came out into the open, that they were among at least a dozen positive witnesses of the phenomenon.

The phantom bus was invariably seen driving fast at the dangerous junction of St Mark's Road and Cambridge Gardens, where there had been many fatal accidents. The borough council had recently removed the corner of a garden to give motorists better visibility. At normal times of the day drivers travelling along Cambridge Gardens, a quiet residential road leading out of Ladbroke Grove, unless familiar with the district were totally unprepared for the number seven buses that turned quickly out of St Mark's Road into Cambridge Gardens, and there had been many near shaves.

At night the junction took on a chilling aspect as drivers began to tell of their surprise at seeing a bus travelling fast down St Mark's Road at one in the morning, and how, on swerving violently to avoid it, they had looked round to find no bus there at all. At that time of night all the regular buses had stopped running.

Further evidence of the phantom came when a car crashed into the wall of a house on the corner of Cambridge Gardens. Again this occurred at about one in the morning, the dazed driver telling those who rushed out to his aid that he had been travelling along Cambridge Gardens when he suddenly saw a bus drive fast round the corner. He swerved to avoid it, hitting the wall, yet when he turned to look after the bus there was no vehicle to be seen.

A mechanic at nearby St Andrew's Garage then disclosed that several puzzled motorists had told him of their personal encounters with the phantom bus. He added that one night the foreman and an assistant were on duty at the garage when the foreman saw a bus out in front, evidently wanting petrol, and called to the assistant to attend to it. But the mystified assistant came back to say that the bus had gone.

During the next few months several more people reported seeing the ghost bus. Then in June the following year, at a Paddington inquest, it was strongly suggested that the apparition was the cause of a night collision between two cars at the junction. One of the drivers involved, not an inexperienced road user, died in the crash; the other driver, and a pedestrian who had paused at the junction and saw the crash, both said that the dead man, driving a small car, had suddenly and for no apparent reason accelerated as if wanting to get quickly across the junction; the larger car was unable to avoid him and they struck bumpers, after which the small car veered off, crashed into a lamp-post, overturned and burst into flames. There was no other traffic about at the time.

The inquest court now heard how the dangerous junction was firmly believed to be haunted by the phantom bus; how hundreds of people in North Kensington talked about the apparition and dozens claimed to have seen it; how on nights after the regular bus service had stopped, people living there had been awakened by the roar of a bus coming down the street and rushed to the window to see a brilliantly lighted double-decker bus approaching with no visible driver or passengers. According to all the witnesses, the bus went careering to the corner of Cambridge Gardens and St Mark's Road, then vanished completely.

Was it a late staff bus? A glistening reflection of car headlamps from a pillar box on rainy nights? These and many other explanations were put forward, but none was sound. The phantom, according to witnesses, appeared a few more times before stopping its one o'clock run, by which time it had proved beneficial in one respect at least, drawing the serious attention of the authorities to a road blackspot.

Only three years earlier a strange, ghostly motor coach had been said to make an appearance in the East Riding of Yorkshire, though this seemed to be linked with a recent tragic holiday crash. This occurred on Garrowby Hill in August 1931, when a coach travelling from Bridlington to Liverpool collided with a car and crashed into a tree; two people were killed and twenty injured. During the late autumn rumours spread that the lonely road was haunted by a spectral vehicle which appeared out of the darkness travelling silently at enormous speed. It seemed by all accounts to appear only on moonless nights or when there was fog over the countryside, though the motorists who encountered it were in no doubt about its ghostly reality and strongly rejected the theory that it could be a trick of the mists. A series of incidents on the road

seven years of age, had a very pretty face with a very intent expression about it, and golden-brown hair."

The girls separately described to the doctor in charge of the laboratory what they had seen. One of them shortly afterwards found herself affected by a strange influence in other rooms of the building, and the result was that a woman medium was asked to investigate the laboratory, being told only that there seemed to be an unusual atmosphere present in the buildings.

In a room on the top floor the medium said she felt an air of "great distress", while in the guinea-pig house she immediately felt "as if all my physical power drained out of me, and left me helpless"; she was convinced, she said, that something tragic had happened in the place. When, for the first time, she was told what the girls had seen, the medium said that whoever it was they saw had been hurt very badly, but was not dead when she entered the building. The medium believed that a great tragedy had happened, probably in the room upstairs, and the person involved had been brought or came down to the former mortuary in great distress, and died there.

Was it the pretty nurse who had died tragically, some time in the past? A search of the hospital records was an impossible task with such little evidence to go on, and so the golden-haired apparition remains unidentified, just one more among the many nameless ones.

I

LOCKED UP TO DIE

In 1944 a young London girl was evacuated to a big old house near the village of Woburn Sands, on the Buckinghamshire-Bedfordshire border. On her arrival a temporary bed was put up for her in the drawing room. What happened next is best described from a statement she made three years afterwards.

"In the night I awoke and saw hands and arms coming out of the wall above my head. I felt somewhat aghast. However, I must have dropped off to sleep, but some time later I again woke up and saw the hands and arms once more coming out of the wall.

"Afterwards I felt much more disturbed by what I had seen than I did at the time. I felt that I could not possibly sleep in that room again. I moved to another room and I never again saw anything uncanny."

The girl's ghostly experience might have remained one of those isolated incidents that occur so frequently but are seldom told outside the family circle, had not the owner of the house in 1947 claimed a reduction in its rateable value, on the ground, among others, that it was haunted.

The owner of the house, "Woodfield", in Weathercock Lane was Mr B. Key of Twickenham, who told the Luton Area Assessment Committee that the house had fallen in value because it was said to be haunted by the ghosts of two lovers who were locked in a cupboard and left to die by the girl's angry father some 250 years ago. Their skeletons, he said, were claimed to have been discovered by Dick Turpin when seeking refuge there, and the highwayman had agreed to keep silent at the promise of sanctuary at "Woodfield" whenever he needed it. The house had stood empty for many years before World War II because no one would buy or occupy a property with its reputation.

Mr Key's case was listened to with particular interest by Mr H. W. M. Richards, a member of the assessment committee and also a Dunstable borough councillor. In the general air of high scepticism which greeted the owner's claim, Mr Richards suggested to his committee colleagues that the fairest way to settle the matter would be to visit the house and test the validity of the supposed haunting. He undertook to arrange such an investigation entirely on his own responsibility and report his findings to the committee. This was agreed.

Mr Richards planned his investigation with care and at no cost to the ratepayers. A medium approved by the Psychic Research Board was chosen for a seance at "Woodfield", and at midnight on a Friday in September, 1947 eight people sat with linked hands in the darkened room where the young evacuee had seen the groping hands emerge from the wall. They included, along with Mr Richards, Mrs Florence Thompson, a London medium, Mr Peter Craven, her assistant, and several newspapermen.

The night passed uneventfully except for one brief interlude when the medium went into a trance. In a distressed voice she then began repeating, "You're killing me . . . stop tying me up . . . let me go . . . I want to go away . . . ." For some minutes the others sat in silence while the medium moved her arms agitatedly and could be heard sobbing, saying she had been shot in the head. After regaining control she complained of violent pains in one side of her head and, pointing to one corner of the room, said she felt sure that a terrible love tragedy had taken place there. There were indications of two spirits who were in need of help, one of them a girl of about twenty-two, and she thought that a seance by a "rescue circle" would release them.

During the seance the sole occupier of the house, Miss Amy Dickinson, who had put up the young evacuee, sat awake in her room. She dismissed newspapermen's questions about the ghosts, saying she had heard tales but was not the nervous type.

Mr Richards felt that the seance had shown there was some influence present, but he was not fully satisfied and decided to hold another seance, before reporting back to his committee. This was held a fortnight later, again on a Friday night, and besides Mrs Thompson and her assistant Mr Craven, another approved medium, Mr George Kenneth, was present; also Dr Donald West, of the Society for Psychical Research.

This second seance produced much more result, two of the sitters claiming to have seen the ghostly face of an old man moving about the darkened room. One of them, Mr Craven, said the face was "an awful greyish colour"; the old man appeared at the side of Mr Kenneth and seemed to be trying to whisper in the medium's ear. Mr Kenneth afterwards told the circle that he saw a tremendous black horse in the room, and heard screams at the beginning of the seance. He also saw an elderly man with a long beard, who looked like a farmer.

Mrs Thompson, while under trance, "contacted" a young girl

who said her name was Bessie and gave the name of her lover as John. Mrs Thompson said the girl was about twenty and very beautiful; her lover was gaunt and dark. The girl told her, "We were going away together, but my father knew, and hurt my head. We have been shut away a long time . . . help John for me . . . help us to rest." The medium said she had the impression of being bound and helpless, and she was certain there had been a double tragedy in the room.

There was some disappointment that nothing had come through the seances that could be firmly checked, or that was over and above what was already known. Mr Richards had hoped they might be given some indication of the burial place of the lovers' skeletons after their discovery in the cupboard by Turpin. But he was now fairly satisfied that the house was haunted and told the assessment committee as much at their next meeting, when he described his investigations at "Woodfield" in full. He then stood down while his colleagues considered their decision. After little deliberation they rejected the owner's claim.

The events at "Woodfield" had by now created such interest that requests were received from people all over the country asking to be allowed to attend a seance. Their requests could not be entertained, but Mr Richards, undaunted by the committee's verdict, decided to hold a third and final seance, and at this the spirit girl "Bessie" again controlled the medium, Mrs Thompson, asserting that she had been killed by her father, and that "John" was with her. Two of the sitters claimed to see manifestations clairvoyantly.

"Woodfield's" owner, Mr Key, lodged an appeal against the assessment committee's ruling. But this went through for consideration on other grounds than that of the ghosts; and so one of the few semi-official investigations into a haunting remained, as far as the local authority's records were concerned, "not proven".

More than ten years earlier, in 1936, ghosts had brought another house owner to court over her rates, though on this occasion not to claim depreciation of the property but absolute financial ruin because of the hauntings.

Mrs Florence Hilda Loury bought Enborne House, an isolated, tree-girt property two miles from Newbury, Berkshire, through a mortgage with a building society, and without any capital except a small grant from a relative, set out to establish it as a guest house. The big old Victorian building was built on the site of a much older mansion dating from the days of Cromwell, parts of which remained. It was not without a certain appeal, especially to the

visitor from town, but Mrs Loury had not been there long before
she found the house was always full of noises, some explainable but
others not. Soon her guests began to complain of hearing strange
clanking sounds in the night; some were so frightened that they
had to leave. One girl was so upset by the weird noises that she
quit the house at once, on the verge of a nervous breakdown.

Mrs Loury herself saw the noisy ghost, that of an old man bent
almost double with age, with his hands and feet shackled, walking
slowly down a dark corridor. He vanished in a moment. A kennel
boy left alone in the house for a time also saw the old man
shuffling down a passage. When the other occupants returned
they found the boy sitting huddled up, petrified with fright; all he
could do was gasp "I have seen a ghost . . .".

It seemed clear that the noises were being caused by the old man
moving through the bedrooms in his chains. Mrs Loury herself
was not afraid of the ghost as she had been in a haunted house
before, but the reputation of Enborne House quickly spread and
soon no guests came at all. Mrs Loury's venture failed and on a
day in September, 1936 she found herself at Newbury police court,
summoned for non-payment of rates. It was then she told the
magistrates the full story of her ruination by the ghost.

By this time the house had been resold, soon to be taken over by
its new owner, a Southampton surgeon, and Mrs Loury, all her
money gone, had had to take a post elsewhere as a housekeeper.

Just who the ghost was who had brought about her failure
nobody knew. There was a tradition in the locality that a beautiful Newbury girl was murdered at Enborne House by her lover in
a fit of jealousy 200 years ago, but the identity of the old man
remained a mystery. Further evidence of the hauntings came from
several people including Lady Hewett, a friend of Mrs Loury's,
who told of how she had talked to people who had heard the
ghostly noises in the night—chains clanking and doors banging—
and had no doubt they were genuinely frightened. An alert
reporter of the *Sunday Referee* who kept watch all night for a sight
of the old man in chains had a fright himself when he saw something for which he had not been looking. At about 4.15 am., when
glancing from an upstairs window at the silent lawn and hedges
probably little changed since the murder two centuries before, he
saw a bush tremble, and for a fleeting instant a slim, shadowy form
seemed to come into view. He could not see a face but had an
impression of a wide skirt and two hands. The lonely figure turned
a corner of the house and vanished in the direction of the stables.

The presence of one more ghost did not deter the new owner,
who said he would not lose any sleep over them; and in fact no

more visitations were reported once the guest house was re-occupied as a private home.

And Mrs Loury? After establishing that she had not received a penny profit from the resale of the house, the sympathetic magistrates decided that if she paid off the rates by weekly instalments, they would reduce the £40 she owed by half.

The sympathy of a court of a different nature was asked for in 1933, when, during the days of depression and high unemployment, a man who abruptly left a job found for him in South Wales had to show cause why his dole money should not be stopped.

The events leading up to this unusual case began when the man, an unemployed baker of Llangollen, Denbighshire, obtained through the local employment exchange a job in the mining village of Glyncorrwg, a hundred-odd miles to the south, near Port Talbot. He made his way there as instructed and began work at the old Glyncorrwg Bakery on the night of his arrival. Nothing unusual happened then, but on the second night, shortly after midnight, he heard weird tappings on the bakehouse window, and on the third night he felt a sudden draught as if someone was passing him hurriedly.

The climax came on the fourth night. While busy kneading he heard strange noises in the room next to the bakery and, looking up, saw the door open and an elderly woman wearing a black dress "waft in". She looked him straight in the face and then vanished. He was so shocked that he staggered back, nearly knocking over his mate, who, though he had not seen the ghost, had felt the draught.

The baker packed up at once and returned to North Wales, where he was threatened with stoppage of his unemployment pay for walking out of his job without good reason. He appeared before the Court of Referees at Wrexham, who listened to the detailed explanation of his ghostly experience, his testimony being supported by a statement written out for him by the owner of the Glyncorrwg Bakery, who admitted that many journeymen who worked there in the past had claimed to have seen the unknown lady in black, though he himself had never encountered her.

The baker's obvious sincerity impressed the court, who directed that his unemployment pay should be suspended for one week only. Meantime, at Glyncorrwg a night's vigil in the old bakery proved fruitless. But older villagers recalled a sensation of thirty years ago when a ghost was seen several times in the village, in the churchyard, and in a cottage on the hillside. This, too, was an unknown "lady in black" who vanished as mysteriously as she came.

THE TEN OF DIAMONDS

There are some strange incidents that are unique in their circumstances and do not fall readily into any ghostly category. Such are the following three stories which involve respectively a playing card, a common kitchen chair, and a used food tin.

The first incident comes from Dorset in the 1920s.

In the little village of Leigh lived Mr Herbert Faulkener, a man who had given up the ambition of becoming a surgeon and taken to a country life. His wife came from Frome, in Somerset. She was the only child of Mr Percy Benjamin Newport, a butcher in Frome for many years, who eventually came to live with the couple at Leigh. Mr Newport was in indifferent health, and though still only in his fifties had to spend his mornings in bed.

One morning in the first week of January, 1927, while busy with her housework, Mrs Faulkener heard her father cry out upstairs. She hurried up to find him sitting up in bed, gazing intently before him.

"Look, look!" he cried. "That nurse! She has a black pot with hot, steaming stuff in it. And a card, the ten of diamonds. Take it away from her—take it away. She is threatening me—she'll empty the boiling stuff over my head if you don't take the card away."

Mrs Faulkener was unable to see either the nurse or the ten of diamonds. She tried to soothe her father but he persisted for some time, moaning "Take the card away from her and that will save me."

Eventually Mrs Faulkener managed to coax her father round to a calmer state of mind, and later on he dressed and came downstairs.

He then said to her, "Don't think I'm silly, but"—pointing to a pack of cards on the table—"I wish you would take the ten of diamonds out and burn it. I can't get it away from my eyes."

His daughter laughed away his fears and said she would not do anything so silly.

Next day Mr Newport returned to Frome to enter the Victoria Hospital for an operation. He died in the hospital exactly ten days afterwards.

The funeral took place from his brother's house in Frome. The coffin was carried out of the house and placed on a bier on the garden path; it was a walking funeral, and the chief mourners filed out of the house to take their places in the cortege. They were led by Mr Faulkener, the son-in-law, and the dead man's brother. As the two men took their places next to the bier Mr Faulkener happened to look down at the ground, and there, beneath the head of the coffin, lay a playing card. It was the ten of diamonds.

Mr Faulkener, greatly surprised, nudged the elbow of his companion—who knew nothing of the dead man's sight of the nurse with her black pot—and he, too, plainly saw the card lying on the path. Neither man wanting to disturb the funeral procession they left the card where it was, but when they searched for it shortly afterwards it had vanished. Yet during the interval no one had been in the garden.

The extraordinary sequel came at the Faulkeners' home at Leigh soon afterwards, when the couple were visited by the dead man's brother. A game of cards was suggested, and it was decided to open a new pack. On the seal being broken and the cards checked, one was found to be missing. The ten of diamonds.

The Faulkeners could give no clue to the mystery, which coincidence alone could scarcely explain. The dead man had been very fond of playing cards at home, but he had had no belief at all in psychic phenomena.

The second unusual story comes from the West Riding of Yorkshire in 1933. Following a rumour in the locality of Wharfedale, on the edge of the wind-swept moors, a reporter of the *Sunday Referee* traced a woman who kept a small farm single-handed, and who admitted to a strange haunting that had troubled her, giving the circumstances of it on condition that, to preserve her solitude, her name should not be disclosed.

The land and buildings of the farm had been in the woman's family for 400 years, and on the bare stone floor of the kitchen, the style of which had not changed since the days of the Brontes, the reporter was shown the object of the haunting, a wooden chair.

The woman told him that when her father was alive they both frequently heard a strange noise shortly after midnight, as of a blow being struck against wood. Next morning they would find the chair turned round, with its seat to the wall. Since the death of her father she had caught the chair performing its weird and frightening trick in broad daylight.

"My brother paid me a visit one day," she said, "and in the afternoon while sitting in the kitchen, we heard a scraping noise.

Suddenly we saw the chair begin to turn. It was horrible. My brother had long hair; it rose on his head like the bristles on a new broom. I never believed human hair did stand on end until I saw him.

"I was stiff with fright by the time the chair had stopped, with its seat to the wall. But my brother seized it and flung it out into the lane. 'We're not having that horrible thing in here', he shouted, and went for the axe. But I stopped him. I live alone, and was afraid of what might happen if he broke it."

So the old chair stood again in its corner, sharing the lonely life of the woman whose only living companions were her dogs and cattle.

The third odd story comes from South Devon and concerns what must be one of the queerest ghosts on record: a "bewitched" tin. Its strange and frightening behaviour brought near chaos to a little cottage in the village of Malborough occupied by Mr F. H. Bridle, a labourer, together with his wife and their seven-year-old adopted daughter.

It was just an ordinary Ovaltine tin in which Mr Bridle used to keep his tobacco, and he had had it for a long time, which made its sudden weird antics all the more distressing.

The incidents began one day in February, 1934, as the family were sitting quietly in their old cottage. After taking some tobacco out of the tin Mr Bridle replaced it on the kitchen table, but as he turned his back he heard a crash and, looking round, saw the tin on the floor. Puzzled, he put it back on the table, this time behind several other articles, but it jumped over these and crashed again to the floor. Once more, still unbelieving, he replaced the tin on the table, but again it leapt over the other articles and dropped to the floor.

This unnerved him and he gingerly looked inside the tin, but saw only tobacco. He cautiously placed the tin inside another, larger tin and stood this in the centre of another table in the room, but he had scarcely turned away before there was a loud crash and the big tin was on the floor with the Ovaltine tin rolling out of it.

Now quite distressed, Mr Bridle and his wife decided to put the tin away out of sight in a cupboard, fastening the cupboard door on its button catch. But to their amazement the door burst open and the tin came sailing through the air. So violently did the cupboard door open that it crashed against the chair on which Mrs Bridle was sitting, striking her on the ribs with such force that she cried out. Her husband quickly seized the Ovaltine tin and thrust it into a drawer which he slammed shut—but the drawer was forced open as if by unseen hands and out jumped the tin again.

"Uncanny and terrible" was how the bewildered couple after-wards described this fantastic episode, but there was much more to come.

Mr Bridle grabbed the tin and took it to an outhouse some yards from the cottage, where he put it inside and securely fastened the door. The relieved couple now thought themselves to be safely rid of the tin, but when Mr Bridle had been back in the cottage only a short time they heard a noise at the door. Their small daughter opened it to greet the unexpected caller, and in a flash the tin came in through the doorway "like a bird going through the air" and, turning to the right into the kitchen, moved across the floor towards Mr Bridle.

In order to get to the front door the tin had had to go right round the outside of the cottage. When the couple ran out and examined the outhouse door they found it still securely fastened.

With the tin now quiet, Mrs Bridle and her daughter went up to undress. But no sooner had they got to the bedroom than the tin came flying up the stairs to stop with a crash on a small table. When they left the bedroom it came down the stairs after them; then again it was quiet.

All that night the uneasy couple heard the tin rattling as it moved about downstairs. Mrs Bridle, thoroughly frightened, sus-pected that her family were "ill-wished" by someone in the village and the tin's antics were the result. She told her husband she would not have the tin in the house any longer, so in the morning he took it with him to work, placing it on a hedge in view of himself and his workmates. It did not move an inch all day. However, as he could not take it home again he gave it to another of the workmen. This man, when the tin still did not move, lost interest and gave it to someone else, and it was this third party whom a reporter of the *Western Evening Herald* finally tracked down to get possession of the Ovaltine tin, whose behaviour had now attracted the attention of a wider public. The reporter took the tin home and slept with it by his bedside, but it never once moved from its position during the night.

The tin's short, hectic career remained a mystery, though as some people suggested, probably the tin itself was not to blame but was made to perform the frightening tricks by some ghostly pre-sence or poltergeist in the Bridles' 200-year-old cottage. Whatever the cause, with the tin out of the house the family were not troubled again.

LIVING WITH A GHOST

One evening in 1933 Mr Allan Hall glanced out of the window of his large house in the mining village of Forest Hall, near New-castle-on-Tyne, and to his surprise, as there were no callers expected, saw a "man in grey" emerge from the semi-darkness and walk up the drive leading to the house. Mr Hall went immediately to the front door, but on opening it found no one there.

A few days later the same mysterious grey figure reappeared, this time in daylight. And so began the long haunting of Rose Villa, which had been built on the site of a former mansion, Forest Hall, from which the village took its name.

During the next three years Mr Hall, his wife and daughter, and friends of the family all saw the ghostly man in grey walk up the driveway of the house at various times. The figure always came the same way, walking to the house and disappearing behind it, and the family eventually became quite accustomed to it and began to refer to it as "Our friend"; it seemed to be quite a friendly ghost and never frightened anyone. Mr Hall, an undertaker, often used to stand at the window and watch for the spectre to make its appearance.

The Halls lived quite happily with their ghost for three years until December, 1936 when news of the apparition finally leaked out and was published in various newspapers. Then, so many sight-seers swarmed to Rose Villa and stood outside it day and night, watching for the apparition, that police had to be called to control them. The ghost, hardly surprisingly, chose not to appear for the crowds.

Local tradition was that a subterranean passage once connected the old Forest Hall mansion with Seaton Delaval Hall, some three miles away, and this inspired the suggestion that the "man in grey" might be the spirit of the famous Delaval monk of Tyne-mouth Priory, who, centuries ago, calling at Seaton Delaval Hall for food to feed the poor, carried away a boar's head ready to be served and was slain by Lord Delaval for the theft. Alternatively it was suggested the ghost was some other uneasy spirit from the subterranean passage, or a vault, the entrance to which was believed to lie under a huge moss covered stone slab in the grounds

of Rose Villa. The slab was only a few feet from the drive where
the "man in grey" was regularly seen to walk. Excitement ran so
high that police had to restrain over eager sightseers who ran into
the grounds to examine the mysterious stone slab.

Mr Hall had never attempted to raise this stone and he now made
it quite clear that he had no intention of disturbing it in any way;
in fact he had no desire to lay the ghost. So the numbers of sightseers and visitors gradually dwindled until all became quiet again
at Rose Villa, leaving the family in peace with their friendly
spectre.

A ghost outside the house is one thing, having it permanently
about inside the building is another, as Mr Edwin Tugwood and
his wife found on taking over the grocery store in the tiny Wiltshire
village of Steeple Ashton. Yet after the first shocks they also
managed to live with their spectre quite well.

Mr Tugwood and his wife, having spent most of their lives
farming in Kent, bought the store at Steeple Ashton in 1944. The
little shop formed part of a fine old timbered cottage with dark oak
beams and heavy iron-latched doors, which in the reign of James
II (1685-9) had been used as the village courthouse.

Mr and Mrs Tugwood were told of rumours concerning the
centuries-old building immediately they moved into it. Customers
spoke of how it was reputed to be haunted by a ghost in an upstairs
cupboard; it was believed to be the ghost of "Bloody" Judge
Jeffreys, who had held circuit courts in a large upstairs room.

The Tugwoods, who had no belief in ghosts, dismissed the
stories. They heard creaking at night and doors opened and
banged, but they expected such noises in a building of that great
age. As for the former courtroom, Mrs Tugwood used it as a
sitting room and kept the four oaken cupboards in it closed,
because she had seen black spiders in them and she had a horror
of spiders. She did notice one odd thing, however. The corner
cupboard, a pigeon-holed one, was often found open in the
morning.

They had been two years in the store when Mrs Tugwood
decided to change their living arrangements and turn the old
courtroom into a bedroom. It was immediately after this that the
ghostly incidents began.

One night as she was standing by the window side of the room,
preparing for bed, with her husband already asleep, she heard
footsteps on the landing outside. Then the iron latch of the bedroom door was lifted, the door pushed open, and the latch released
again, as though by a human hand. She waited, expecting her
daughter to appear, but instead to her horror saw a "cloaked

shadow" pass from the door across to the corner cupboard, making a heavy tread as it walked, and open the cupboard door and search the pigeon-holes, as though for missing papers. As soon as the thing's back was turned she dived into bed and under the clothes, too frightened even to wake her husband. She remembered how it was said that Judge Jeffreys had used this cupboard for filing his papers.

Her husband, when she told him next day of her experience, was sceptical but sympathetic, believing she had perhaps been working too hard. But three months later Mr Tugwood both saw and heard the ghost himself, so clearly that he flung a heavy shoe at it; but the shoe passed right through the cloaked figure and only succeeded in cutting a piece of plaster from the wall, the ghost continuing uninterrupted on its way to the cupboard.

After this the ghost paid frequent, if irregular, visits in which it climbed the stairs, walked along the passage, lifted the heavy latch on the door and, walking across the bedroom to the old oak cupboard, searched among the pigeon-holes. Relatives who came to scoff at the spectre stayed, saw it, and left convinced of its existence. One evening a nephew of the couple in his twenties, who had been more sceptical than most, rushed downstairs "with his hair on end", shouting hysterically that he had seen the ghost. He said he had heard it walk the passage and seen the door open as it entered the old courtroom.

The Tugwoods had to decide whether to give in to the ghost and quit the cottage, or to stay and put up with it. Mr Tugwood reasoned that it seemed harmless enough and appeared to have no objection to their presence, so they would stay. The couple made one change. As Mrs Tugwood could not stand the noisy way in which the ghost opened the bedroom door, with a sudden clang of the latch, they slept in future with the door open to allow it easy admittance.

Several tenants of a farm near Watford, Hertfordshire, were driven away by its ghost before a couple arrived who learned to live with it. The ghost was said to be that of a little old woman in a black gown with white lace, who was seen wandering around the ancient buildings of Green End Farm. She was never threatening, but was apparently responsible for waking people in the night by pulling off the bedclothes.

Strange noises, too, were heard at the farm: the sound of a whining dog, the jingle of harness, and hurried footsteps, seemingly clattering over cobbles outside. The history of the sound of horses was believed to go back to 1642, when Cromwell quartered some of his Roundheads in the attic.

Local villagers, as well as the farmhouse occupants, heard the various noises right up to the late 1940s, though the cobbles had been removed some twenty years before.

There was no explanation for the lady in black. No one knew who she was; no bones had been found, and there was no record of any person dying violently at the farm. Some people believed that to see the ghost was a warning of disaster. Mr Herbert Simmonds, a former tenant, told how his brother was awakened night after night by the old lady who beckoned him to follow her, but he never did. Soon afterwards he was drowned. A woman visitor to the farm also saw the lady in black just before her husband was killed.

But Mr and Mrs David Keeble, on moving in, believed the ghost to be perfectly harmless and they liked her happy smile. The first night was a shock for Mrs Keeble. "I shall never forget it—it was horrible, especially the sounds outside," she told the *Empire News* in September, 1950. "But now I don't mind. The old lady seems happy with us. She not only appears at night; during the day I meet her on the stairs or when I am cooking. Sometimes I feel she is the rightful owner and I am only the guest."

An unusual haunting has gone on for some years in a house at West Tisted, Hampshire. Commander John F. Baird, a retired naval commander and his family, call the ghost "George". They have never seen "him", but he smokes foul tobacco, which the family usually smell in the kitchen or on the stairs. A cloud of tobacco smoke is also seen on occasions. Mrs Baird had an early shock when, on seeing it blowing about in the garden, she realised suddenly that the smoke was blowing in the opposite direction to the wind. At other times the mysterious smoke has inexplicably blown in her face.

But, she tells me, "There is nothing sinister about 'George'. He seems a very benign and well intentioned presence."

The family believe "George" to be the ghost of a French prisoner, as apparently some prisoners were kept there during the Napoleonic wars. Part of the house is some 400 years old, and at least one old French coin has been unearthed there.

THE GHOST OF WOOKEY HOLE

Wookey Hole Caves, a series of underground caverns at the foot of the Mendip Hills in Somerset, are the oldest known home of man in Britain. They were also, according to local legend, the home a thousand years ago of the Witch of Wookey, an evil woman whose activities put a blight on the district. A monk of Glastonbury had to be called to exorcise her, and for her persistent wickedness he turned her into stone. A black stalagmite formation which rises in striking profile beside the underground river in Wookey Hole is said to be the witch's frozen effigy.

So much for the legend, which has been passed down through generations in the nearby village of Wookey Hole and surrounds. In this century, just as numerous excavations have proved the existence in the caves of early British tribes, so they would seem in addition to give added strength to the legend of the witch. For during excavations in 1912 there was found, at a depth of ten feet, the skeleton of a young woman, together with a dagger, knife, weaving comb and ball of white stalagmite resembling a witch's crystal; and beside her, the bones of two goats.

Fifteen years later, in 1927, Wing Commander Gerard Hodgkinson, whose family had owned Wookey Hole and the land round about for hundreds of years, began to develop the witch's "lair" as a public attraction. Gardens leading up to the caves were created, and a museum, shops and restaurant added as the enterprise was gradually built up into the showplace of the Mendips it is today, with the legendary Witch of Wookey becoming known throughout the world.

With this evocative background it is not to be wondered at that in the late 1940s, when uncanny incidents began to occur in a cottage on the Wookey Hole estate, some people thought it might be due to the witch having returned to start her strange tricks again. Certainly there were few places more suggestive of the darkly supernatural where a ghost could have chosen to appear.

The haunted cottage itself had no previous ghostly history. Built in the 1870s, it had been lived in for almost the whole of her life by a woman who died there in 1947, aged over eighty. She had declined to have electricity installed in the cottage, so this work was done after her death. It was then the hauntings began.

A couple with a young son took over the tenancy of the cottage temporarily. One evening the eight-year-old boy, who had gone upstairs, came down looking very frightened and asked his mother, "Who is that old lady in the white apron upstairs?" His puzzled mother went back upstairs with him to investigate and was shocked to see the ghost of an old woman walk across the landing. After this upsetting incident the family repeatedly heard phantom footsteps going up and down the stairs, and saw the old woman's ghost several more times. It was too much for them and they moved out.

But the hauntings did not stop with the family's departure. Instead, over the next few years it got progressively worse, until it became impossible to get people to stay in the cottage. The footsteps continued their eerie tread, as if someone was walking about upstairs, though whenever anyone went up to look there was no one there. Doors bulged with pressure and flew open and shut, electric lights switched themselves on and off in the middle of the night, and things moved from place to place. The ghost, in a mob cap and white apron, continued to walk, accompanied always by a wave of intense cold and a dead, dank smell.

When the cottage, together with the one adjoining, was taken over for use by catering staff at the Cave Restaurant, a terrified woman employee who slept there saw the ghost step through the wall into her bedroom.

The restaurant manageress at the time, who had no belief in ghosts, then agreed to sleep in the cottage; but after only a short time in the building she felt very uneasy and could not sleep. She went for the assistant manageress and together the two women searched the cottage but found nothing wrong. The manageress went back to bed. At 2 am., however, she awoke with the chilling sensation of a cold hand on her shoulder, and, sitting up in bed, was horrified to see the ghost walk through the doorway. As on previous occasions the old woman's apparition was accompanied by "a smell like death itself".

By the summer of 1952 the hauntings in the cottage had continued at intervals for nearly five years, and Mrs Olive Hodgkinson, wife of Wookey Hole's owner, had evidence from a total of twenty-three people who had experienced the ghost, seven of whom had actually seen it. She decided that something would have to be done about it.

A psychical research investigator held a vigil in the cottage. This proved fruitless; nevertheless the incidents still went on. The help of the vicar of Wookey Hole was then sought, and in 1954 a service of blessing and prayers was held in the building.

The vicar's service was entirely successful. Mrs Hodgkinson tells me that there were no further disturbances and staff have lived in the cottage quite happily since.

So a thousand years after the sudden end of the Witch of Wookey, a second alarming spectre had been laid.

K

THE CRIME OF JOHN CARVER

The haunting of an old timbered cafe on the outskirts of Croydon, Surrey, in the 1940s brought echoes of a strange murder trial held nearly eighty years before; one which, because of its curious circumstances must be among the oddest cases in English criminal records.

The events leading up to the trial of John Carpenter Carver, in 1870, began early one day in May of that year.

Carver, an upholsterer and furniture dealer in his thirties, lived with his wife and their year-old baby in a house at South End, Croydon. The house was divided into two and had two small shops under the one roof. Carver rented his half of the premises from the house owner, William Morgan, a builder, who carried on business from one shop while Carver plied his trade in the other. Carver's share of the house consisted of the shop with a small parlour at the back, a bedroom on the first floor and an attic. He employed a young servant girl named Mary Ann Turner.

Carver had been married for ten years. His wife, Anne, was a small, lightly-built woman who apparently had to suffer a lot from her husband's bitter tongue. He was often heard to quarrel with her, using abusive language, and even to threaten her, and she was known to have fits of hysterical sobbing.

On this May morning Carver was heard once again abusing his wife, and in the early afternoon he quarrelled with her again. A man who happened to come to the shop door at about half-past two heard Carver swearing at his wife, while another witness (names were not given in the court reports) told of how he heard Carver suddenly shout in the parlour, "I'll knock your brains out!" This witness said that as he stood watching, Carver appeared to fall from one part of the room towards another. He then saw Carver raise his hands three or four times, as if striking at something violently; but as Carver had nothing in his hands he decided he had better mind his own business, and walked away.

A short time after this Carver went next door to the Morgans and asked them to send for a doctor, as he believed his wife was dead or dying. Mrs Morgan ran into the Carvers' parlour, where she saw Anne Carver lying on the floor quite still, with blood on the upper part of her dress. Mrs Morgan exclaimed to Carver, "Oh, you wretch!" He replied simply, "It was an accident."

The doctor found that a deep knife wound had penetrated Anne Carver's heart, killing her instantly. Carver went for a policeman on duty in South End and brought him to the house. Then, quite calmly, he gave his version of what had happened, during which time large groups of people gathered outside his house and in various streets round about, for the news had travelled quickly.

Carver swore that his wife's death was an accident—"and if I am hung for it I can't help it." He said that on coming home to a dinner of boiled bacon, he went out and cut some mustard and cress which he gave to his wife to wash. She did so, and then served it up to him on a plate from which the servant girl had just had her meal. This plate had lain on the top of two other plates, which were clean. Carver said he remonstrated with his wife for giving him his dinner on the dirty plate. They quarrelled and she aggravated him so much that he flung all three plates at the wall and smashed them. This made his wife "savage" and she flew at him with great violence, just as he was cutting some bacon. The impact knocked him over a chair with his back to the wall, and he was transfixed there with the knife and fork held forward in his hands. While he was in this position his wife again rushed at him and fell against the extended knife.

He said he did not realise at first what had happened. His wife turned round, walked across the little room and sat down in a chair, but then fell off it, as he thought in a fainting fit, into the fireplace. He lifted her out of the fireplace on to the floor, and only then discovered that she had been wounded and appeared to be dying. He went for the Morgans.

Carver was taken through the crowds to the police station where, when charged with the wilful murder of his wife, the *Croydon Times* noted "he exhibited great coolness. He made a statement with the utmost deliberation, and after it was read over to him, he dictated some verbal alterations."

The trial was held at Guildford Assizes that August. A doctor agreed that Anne Carver, small as she was, could have received the fatal wound just as described by the husband, even though it was inflicted by a common table knife with a rounded end and not one with a sharp point.

Carver's counsel then submitted there was no case for the jury to consider, but the judge, after a short deliberation, said he "thought" he ought not to stop the case. So Carver's counsel briefly addressed the jury, after which the judge summed up and the jury retired, though their verdict seemed to be a foregone conclusion. Carver's counsel endorsed his brief "Not Guilty", handed it to the prisoner's solicitor and left the court.

But the jury returned in half an hour to pronounce Carver "Guilty", though adding that they recommended him to mercy as they thought that his wife, in putting the dirty plate before him, had provoked him. When asked if he had anything to say before sentence of death was passed, Carver strongly challenged the evidence of the witness who claimed to have seen his hands raised, and said he would die happily as he knew he was innocent.

Carver's solicitor, Mr H. Parry, was thunderstruck at the jury's verdict. He wrote to the editor of the *Croydon Times* asking him to inform the public that, following the "extraordinary verdict" he had sent a copy of the depositions to the Home Secretary, urgently requesting him to have inquiries made "for the purpose of obtaining the only reparation that can now be made my unfortunate client—a pardon—which I feel the greatest confidence in obtaining".

Remarking on the trial scene, the solicitor wrote, "While the jury were being conducted by the officer of the court upstairs to the jury-room, a lady in the company of two other ladies of the high-sheriff (all of whom sat on the Bench during the trial), exclaimed audibly, 'Poor fellow, I hope they will not keep him long in suspense.' In fact it was the universal feeling frequently expressed during the absence of the jury that the delay was unnecessary. The verdict caused quite a sensation in the town of Guildford, the universal expression being 'The prisoner ought to have been acquitted.' I don't think a single person in court (and there were several hundreds) excepting the twelve Cobham jurymen, agreed with the verdict."

Three weeks later Carver got his free pardon, and again his solicitor wrote in strong terms to the local newspaper.

"My anticipations have been realised; Carver has been pardoned, and was liberated on Wednesday morning at eleven o'clock. He is pardoned for what? For having the misfortune to be tried by a common jury for the most serious offence known to our criminal law—a jury devoid of common sense and by whom he was found guilty of an offence of which he was innocent."

Mr Parry charged in his letter that there had been prejudice against Carver from the start, from members of the inquest jury.

A month after his release from the condemned cell Carver returned to Croydon. He went first to the police court in the morning to claim some articles which had been taken from him on arrest, including his wife's wedding ring, afterwards saying that he intended to visit his wife's grave and then "look for a fresh place of business". News of his arrival soon spread and he was recognized in the street, carrying a loaded carpet-bag, at which, as *The Times* reported, "A number of women became violent in their demonstrations of disgust and he was pursued by a mob of seven or eight hundred people, who threatened to tear him to pieces."

The hostile crowd followed Carver wherever he went and tried several times to attack him. He was harried up and down the neighbourhood of South End, and on a number of occasions had to flee to a convenient house or hotel to escape assault, eventually being holed up by his increasingly violent pursuers in a house close to the Brighton Road, outside which a huge crowd gathered. The police arrived in force and had to run him out the back way, through the grounds, into the Brighton Road. Eventually, after finding himself still unable to throw off the crowds, he fled to the home of a relative in Purley.

There was no future in Croydon for John Carpenter Carver, the anger of the townsfolk made that plain. And so, slipping into anonymity, he quit the neighbourhood and, some say, the country.

Did his injured spirit return some eighty years later in the 1940s? Miss Hilda Steel, in her cafe on the Brighton Road, was convinced of it. Her cafe was in an old building that went back 200 years in time; massive oak beams supported walls and ceiling, floors were uneven with unexpected steps, and a narrow, twisting staircase led to the rooms above. It was when white-haired Miss Steel tried to sleep in the room immediately above the cafe that strange things occurred during the night. Baking tins rattled in the kitchen and the oven door slammed to and fro. Doors left locked were found wide open in the morning, with the keys hidden behind plates or under tables.

Miss Steel actually saw the ghost, which she described as being a tall, grey form without head or legs. Several of her kitchen staff saw it too. They said the ghost was invariably heralded by an icy blast of air, and that it glided in through the back door, climbed the stairs and hovered on the landing.

Why should Carver's ghost haunt the old cafe? Because it was thought that the cafe building had been one of his refuges when he had run from shelter to shelter in that area to hide from the mob. Added to this supposition was the fact that there was an additional ghostly disturbance in the cafe every year on the night of May 26, the date of his wife's death, when an unaccountable crash and tinkling of glass was heard "as if a heavy body had fallen through a plate glass window".

Yet no one at this time, after the long passage of years, could have known the exact circumstances of the Carvers' fatal quarrel; and certainly they had no knowledge of the incident (only recently brought to light by myself from old records) in which the husband had snatched up all the dinner plates and hurled them against the wall in his rage.

If the ghost, now gone, was Carver's, it would seem that he himself was haunted by the echo of his rash and unfortunate act.

THE ROMAN PATROL

Roman ghosts are not common and the one reported to have walked through the centuries at Mersea Island, Essex, has particular interest, appearing as it does only at times of heavy rains. The ghost is said to be that of a Roman warrior, fully clad in armour, who, when swamping rains threaten The Strood, the old Roman causeway to the mainland, is seen to walk in sorrowful patrol from Barrow Hill to The Strood, where he stands for a moment before gradually fading away.

During the last century and in the early 1900s the ghost, sometimes described by witnesses as having the appearance of a Roman general, was seen on several such stormy nights, with long intervals between. The warrior's last two recorded visits, however, were both made in July, 1939 during a week of heavy rains.

There were at this time many islanders who would not use the East Mersea Road after an appearance by the apparition, and some others who would not on any account use the road after nightfall for fear of meeting the ghostly figure. Among witnesses of the doleful spectre in earlier years was one woman who testified to both seeing and hearing the apparition on several occasions, and there were local historians who felt there was a firm basis for the stories of the haunting, though who the ghost could possibly be was lost in the island's eventful past.

Barrow Hill, the old burial ground from which the ghost was invariably seen to begin its walk was excavated at the turn of the century and Roman remains found; also, a burial chamber of Roman tiles, in which was found a glass urn containing bones, thought to be those of an Essex chieftain. The strong local belief has persisted that the remains of the sorrowing Roman patrol have yet to be discovered, although there have been no further sightings of the ghost since 1939.

Around this same time the sounds of ghostly soldiers of another early era were claimed to be heard close to the ancient moated mounds forming Thunderfield Castle, near Horley, Surrey. The castle is believed to have been a halting place of King Harold's army as it marched to Hastings to meet the invading soldiers of William of Normandy. For countless years there had existed a tradition that a ghostly army was sometimes to be heard marching along a road near the castle.

Early in 1937, some months after the first excavations had begun on the privately owned castle site, a local farmer, Mr F. Godden, and his wife, were surprised to hear at times the tramp of marching feet and the sound of a military voice giving orders, though there was nothing and no one in the vicinity. The noises seemed to issue from mid-air. Then early one night as Mr Godden was driving home in his car, he saw the tall figure of a strange-looking man suddenly appear standing before him in the middle of the road. The man seemed to be wearing a long red cloak and had unkempt fair hair. It was not yet dark and Mr Godden was driving with only his sidelights on. He immediately switched on his headlights and swerved, but the curious figure had vanished.

Other local residents now admitted to hearing the weird sound of tramping feet, as did a friend of Mr and Mrs Godden who came to visit them. The friend, Mr F. E. Jones, who was no believer in ghosts, afterwards described his odd experience while walking along Haroldslea Drive to Mr Godden's house:

"I heard coming towards me a faint, steady tramping of feet. Then as the sound became louder the atmosphere seemed to become icy cold. The sound of the marching became louder until I was in the middle of an invisible company of men. Round me there seemed to be a clink as of metal. Gradually the sound died away.

"It was not imagination; it was something I cannot explain. But it was something very real—yet unreal."

Other people who heard the eerie tramping described it in much the same terms. The burst of ghostly activity by the invisible army seemed to last over several months; then, as at Mersea, all was quiet once more.

ON CANDLEMAS EVE

It is often argued that people see what they want to see, and that impressionable people who have had hauntings described to them sometimes have a "vision" themselves, through imagination or self-suggestion. This is a perfectly valid argument and might perhaps apply in some unsubstantiated cases, but what of the person told of a reputed haunting who unexpectedly witnesses something entirely different?

Such was the experience of Miss Olive Gosden, of Castlemorton, Worcestershire. It happened on the night of February 1, 1940, just a few months after the start of World War II. Miss Gosden, a schoolteacher now retired, describes her uncanny experience:

"A few of us in the village of Colwall, on the Herefordshire side of the Malvern Hills, were running a small club mainly for the village girls and the soldiers camped on the local racecourse, and anyone else who cared to drop in. We were allowed extra rations to run a small canteen, which made it even more popular. I was more or less in charge, and that evening when I got to the club a little after half-past seven I remembered with dismay that extra work at the school nearby, where I taught, had made me forget to fetch our milk supply from a farm about a mile away. So while the others prepared the sandwiches, I seized my bicycle and a big enamelled jug and rode off as fast as I could in the half moonlight, the journey taking me across the village green and down a lonely bit of road which led to a very old sunken lane known as the 'haunted lane'.

"It was told locally how an unfortunate girl who had been turned from her home one snowy night by her brute of a husband had come up that lane with her baby in her arms to ask for shelter from her father, who lived in a house which then stood at the top of the lane. But on her father's orders she was turned away from the door by servants, and was found the next day, drowned in a small quarry pond at the bottom of the lane where the railway now went over a bridge. Her ghost was supposed to be 'seen' coming up the lane.

"Though not naturally nervous I did feel a bit creepy, but saying to myself firmly that my friends at the farm came down there every evening and were none the worse, and that I was not to be a fool, I sped on. There were in fact more earthly things to worry about. The troops had just put up posts with bundles of barbed wire attached beside the lane, and one of these made me jump because it looked like a man, and there was a rumour that German paratroops had been picked up a week before around there. Speeding on I got to the farm by the bridge and collected my milk. Then, feeling much better for a few jokes and their friendly faces, I set off on the return journey. I got back up the 'haunted lane', having to push my cycle most of the way as it was a gradual uphill now, and at the top drew a relieved breath, saying to myself, 'Well, here you are at the top—and it wasn't so bad after all, was it?' Then I gave a loud exclamation of astonishment, for slowly and clearly across the road in front of me I saw a strange small procession of black figures in sweeping black robes.

"I gathered they were cowled monks and got the vivid impression that in their midst they were carrying on a bier the body of a young man who had died away from home. It was all draped in flowing black, and I knew they were carrying him back to his home in the valley and that he had been greatly loved and there would be much sorrow because of his death. It was all quite vividly made known to me, just as if someone stood beside me wordlessly telling me the particulars—or as if I already knew them. I got the impression that the period was about 1400. The procession went slowly on and to my surprise it then seemed to go off down an old track towards the farms in the hollow below. But I had had enough. Terrified by now, I got on my cycle and rode off on the now mercifully downhill way back to the village.

"Then I realised to my horror that what appeared to be a horseman in a cloak and plumed hat was also riding hell for leather at my left hand, as if he, too, were riding away in terror from something he was afraid of. I then seemed to know that he was responsible for the death of the other man and was trying to escape from the knowledge of what had happened. When I looked round the figure did not seem to be there, but directly I looked to my front he was there again, and so we proceeded together all down that lane, round to the left, where he seemed less insistent, and right up the village green until we got to the railway bridge, when it all ceased. But as we came up the green, although the landscape on my left looked the same, in a way it appeared slightly different—at the bridge, where the impression left me, the old road (before the railway was built) led slightly left to an old posting house still standing.

"Feeling very shaken I got back to the club and my friends, more than thankful for the lights. One of them said, 'You *have* been quick.' I laughed and said, 'Yes, I did streak,' and then—'I think I have been haunted in the "haunted lane", but it wasn't where I expected it to be and it wasn't what I was afraid I might see,' describing the exact spot. My friend replied, 'Oh, but that *is* where the men about here say they see things.' I laughed and said, 'It must be an effect of the light there,' feeling quite sure, though, that it was not. It was only the next day, when the old school house-keeper who looked after me mentioned that it was Candlemas Day, that I realised my journey down the lane had been made on Candlemas Eve.

"Some time after I described the incident to an old friend in Malvern, and she told me there was a story that long ago, two young men had fought a duel and the son of the people who lived at a house in the valley had been killed; but whether there is any connection I do not know."

Corroboration can come, much to the relief of a witness, a long time after a ghostly incident. An example of this is the experience of Miss Margery Hookham, of Malvern Wells, who some years ago went with a friend on holiday to a farmhouse in a lonely valley in the north-west of Brecknockshire, in the vicinity of Llanwrtyd Wells.

"In this farmhouse," says Miss Hookham, "I had a large front bedroom, while my friend had a room at the back of the house. I used to wake in the night with my heart thumping, feeling terrified, and sometimes I could hear the sound of someone shuffling about outside my door, which I felt was an old man in slippers. This happened night after night until I quite dreaded going up to bed. Finally my room was changed to one at the back of the house and the feelings I had had, and the sounds I had heard, ceased. All this time my friend had felt and heard nothing.

"Some years afterwards, by the purest coincidence, I met a woman who told me that her sister had stayed at the same farm-house and had exactly the same uncanny experience; a dog she had taken with her nearly went mad with fright and had to be sent away.

"She then told me the story of the house. It was said to be haunted by a horrible old man who used to keep a savage dog and set it to fight all the dogs of the neighbourhood, most of which it killed. The garden when dug up was found to be full of dogs' bones.

"The front bedroom which I had slept in was the haunted room."

Very often corroboration comes much sooner, as in a case at Streatham, London, in 1933. On Christmas night Mr Lewis Amis, of Clapham, a fireman at the newly-built Streatham Astoria had sole charge of the empty theatre, and this was his strange story:

"I was making my round through the darkened theatre shortly after midnight, and as I entered the tea lounge I saw a figure advancing towards me. Thinking it must be a burglar, I turned my torch full on to him and saw the figure of an old man, dressed in a long white gown with a hood over his head, gliding across the floor, his arms held stiffly at his side. I caught a glimpse of a wizened, wrinkled face and short beard, then he turned away from me and moved towards the stairs leading down to the vestibule.

"I followed, and as we reached the doors leading to the stalls they suddenly swung open. The doors are heavy, strongly fastened, and three men would have a job to get them open. The figure glided on down the centre aisle and then leapt, or rather floated, across the orchestra pit, landing behind the footlights in front of the curtain. It now turned and faced me, and, holding its hand aloft, cried in a weird, husky voice, 'I won't sell, I won't sell, I won't sell.' Then it vanished."

Mr Amis's fantastic story was received rather coolly, the kindliest of sceptics dismissing it as a dream. But then came firm evidence to explain the incident. It was discovered that four years before, on the site where the theatre now stood, had lived a Mr James, who, although constant pressure had been brought upon him to sell his pleasant, comfortable house, was loathe to leave it. Eventually he did agree to sell and moved to another part of Streatham, dying soon after. Mr Amis had never heard of Mr James, but the widow confirmed his description of her bearded husband and the fact that Mr James had been very strongly attached to the house and extremely reluctant to give it up so that the site could be developed.

The various ways in which corroboration of a haunting arrives, vouched for by totally independent witnesses, are often as fascinating as the ghostly incidents themselves. The following is a personal example.

In his book *The Midnight Hearse* which I edited, Elliott O'Donnell referred briefly to the spectre said to haunt the Church of St Bartholomew-the-Great in Smithfield, London. This is believed to be the spirit of the monk Rahere, who founded the church together with St Bartholomew's Hospital, the oldest hospital in London, in the twelfth century. Rahere in his early life, as a canon regular of the Order of St Augustine, was a story-teller in the houses of nobles and finally at the court of Henry I. Life at court seems suddenly to have palled, for he plunged himself into penance on a pilgrimage to Rome. On the journey he fell ill and made a vow to St Bartholomew that if he were spared he would devote the rest of his life to the service of the sick poor. He recovered, and returned to fulfil his vow. Granted a site in Smithfield by Henry I, he gathered about him young men and old labourers, and with his hands and theirs raised in 1123 on the site of the present hospital the first "Bart's".

Rahere's apparition is said by many to have been heard and sometimes seen walking along the aisles and ambulatories of St Bartholomew's Church. Elliott O'Donnell however, during a vigil there saw and heard nothing. Now Mrs Isobel Burke tells me from Salisbury, Rhodesia:

"After living in this country (Rhodesia) for some years my mother returned to England in 1928 for a short visit, during which time she saw many old friends. The two incidents I am about to describe happened there shortly before her arrival.

"My mother went first to see a friend who lived in the Midlands —a woman of the world, rich, unmarried and gay—who told my mother she had not been well of late and was full of desperate personal worries. This friend went on to say that one morning on a visit to London she was passing St Bartholomew's and by pure chance and on an impulse decided to go inside for a few minutes. She knelt down in a pew and prayed, her worries being very much on her mind, and was suddenly filled with a sense of peace, together with the feeling that a great burden was being lifted from her. She looked up, and in the pulpit was the figure of a monk in his robes. He looked straight at her and raised his hand in blessing, then slowly descended the steps of the pulpit and walked away. She was much uplifted and described this as a wonderful experience, maintaining that the monk—Rahere—haunted the premises to help people who were in trouble.

"The surprising coincidence came when my mother visited a second friend who lived, I think, in Brighton. She was a highly religious woman, very high church, and rather unworldly. She was in an advanced state of mental anguish and told my mother that her family thought she was—and had accused her of being— deranged, because after a trip to London she told them . . . and here she repeated an almost identical story of seeing the monk as that told to my mother by her other friend, saying also that the sight of the monk had lifted a tremendous burden from her shoulders.

"My mother was able to comfort this woman by telling her of the first friend's experience, so relieving her from the terrible doubt that had been growing in her mind as to whether she had imagined the whole thing. She had gone to the church seeking comfort, unlike the first woman who had acted on a sudden impulse. The two women had never met or even heard of one another and there was an interval of some months between the incidents."

The rector of St Bartholomew's at the time, and his wife, both claimed to have seen the monk, the rector's wife several times.

Mrs Burke adds: "My mother spent the whole of one day there praying, but nothing happened at all, a fact which comforted her to some extent in the belief that her worries (which were of some magnitude) were not so overwhelming that she needed help."

Finally, while considering the various ways in which ghostly incidents are confirmed and explained, it should be noted how very often the clue to an apparently meaningless haunting lies buried in the past.

Many years ago there lived close to the hamlet of Barham, six miles from Canterbury, an illiterate elderly woman who used to wander off at times on walks across the Barham Downs. She knew nothing of the history of the district but often described the things and the people she "saw" during her wanderings. No one took much notice of her fanciful talk, but when in later years her stories came to be considered against the historical background of the Downs they seemed to be very much more than the ramblings of a queer old woman. She had once described how she had been sitting at the back of the Black Mill, near what later was the road to Aylesham, when she saw a body of men marching close together. They wore helmets and "kilts", and she saw the gleam of metal on their uniforms. Yet she knew nothing of the fighting between the Romans and the Britons near the spot.

Another time she told a friend that at a certain place she had seen five ladies in silks and satins dancing with men, who had long curls and feathered hats. Again she knew nothing of the gay life at a camp on this part of the Downs at the time of the Restoration of Charles II.

She also once described seeing a procession of white-robed figures carrying "on a wattle-gate" a great golden image. They passed her slowly, singing as they went, going down into the valley. For this ghostly incident there is as yet no explanation, though from what we have seen it is not unlikely that one will emerge.